ALL CO
HOW TO

DRIVE
FOR THE

THEORY
TEST

PETER HARWOOD

GB

foulsham
LONDON • NEW YORK • TORONTO • SYDNEY

The Publishing House, Bennetts Close,
Cippenham, Berkshire, SL1 5AP, England.

ISBN 0-572-02224-7

Illustrated by Paul Colsell
Typeset by Poole Typesetting (Wessex) Ltd, Bournemouth
Printed in Great Britain by The Westdale Press, Cardiff

CONTENTS

INTRODUCTION

You are about to join the one million hopefuls who want to pass their driving test first time.

Well, the bad news is that half of them will fail, and that's because they don't understand that there are now two important tests to be passed. The good news is that with this book you won't be one of them!

The first test you have to pass is the theory test. Until you are through that, you will not be allowed to be tested on the road. And the theory test is looking for much more knowledge than the straightforward, old Highway Code test. The driving theory test has been introduced so that the testers can examine you in closer detail. In this book, you will find all of the theory which they believe makes drivers safer on the roads.

Their questions aim to find out if you know *why* you need to follow the various driving procedures. They are designed to test your understanding of the principles of good driving.

By reading this book you will gain a firm grip on the principles and the practice of good driving, and from this position you will have nothing to fear from the driving theory test itself.

Most people learn from a professional instructor, which is always the best way to gain a new skill. But that instruction needs to be backed up by study – and that's where books come in. First, read and learn your Highway Code. There is no substitute; but we do have another little book called *The All Colour Highway Code Quiz Book* which is a useful learning tool, in a lighter, more fun, style.!

Some driving books try to talk as though they are your instructor which, of course, they are not. They end up like a good road: dry, flat and good for running cars over!

This book's different. A series of articles rather than a course, it's a reference source as well as a study and revision aid. I hope that the cartoons bring a fun touch to this otherwise serious subject, too.

Remember, driving is easy for anyone who studies and practises a lot, so get to it and good luck.

Some books are good for running cars over

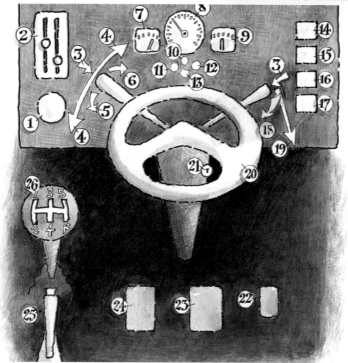

Positions in individual cars may vary

CONTROLS AND INSTRUMENTS

1. Choke: makes fuel mixture richer, for when engine is cold
2. Demister: blows warm air over windscreen, and various other things
3. Horn: only to warn
4. Direction indicators: push the way you intend to turn the wheel
5. Headlight flasher
6. Headlight high beam
7. Fuel gauge
8. Speedometer
9. Engine temperature gauge or light
10. High-beam-on light
11. Ignition light
12. Oil pressure warning light
13. Direction indicator lights: flash with indicators
14. Rear fog-lamps
15. Hazard warning light: all indicators flash
16. Rear window heater: heats window electrically to keep it clear

17. Side/headlights: may be on dashboard. Also works rear lights
18. Windscreen washer: may be on dashboard. Squirts water (at windscreen)
19. Windscreen wipers: may be on dashboard. May have several speeds
20. Steering wheel
21. Ignition/Starter: connects electrical system/turns starter motor
22. Accelerator (or 'gas'): speeds engine by giving it more fuel
23. Foot-brake: slows and stops all four wheels, and works brake light
24. Clutch: separates engine from gearbox, to change gear or slow down
25. Handbrake: positions vary. Fixes back wheels, for parking only
26. Gear lever: lever and gear positions vary

STARTING THE ENGINE

Starting the engine on a cold morning will display your car's most tem-peramental side, but when you get used to its quirks you will be able to do it reliably.

Once you have done your cockpit drill (see right), check the handbrake is on (try pulling it further). Next, check the gear lever is in neutral – it should feel loose if you wobble it sideways. If the engine is cold you will probably need to pull the choke out, unless it is automatic. After starting the engine, push it in a bit, and work it right back during the first minutes of driving.

Switch on the ignition: turn the key until the ignition and oil lights come on. This is usually the second or third position, after releasing the steering lock and the radio. Turn the key further (against a spring) to operate the starter. The starter motor will turn the engine over. When it fires, release the starter immediately.

If the engine does not fire after a few seconds, release the starter, then try again. You may need to hold the accelerator down or pump it, while starting, depending on the car. (Do NOT touch it with an automatic choke on a cold engine.) You may find that it likes different treatment depending on how many attempts you've made. After a few tries you may have flooded the engine. Try operating the starter once with the choke and accelerator off, before trying normally once more. If this doesn't work, give it a long rest.

COCKPIT DRILL

Before you start: check that the doors are properly closed; adjust the seat so you can reach all the controls easily and see clearly; clean and adjust the mirrors; check that all passengers are wearing their seat-belts; check that you have enough fuel for your journey; in an unfamiliar car, find all the controls before you start.

Rather than going on for so long that you run the battery down, it may be a good idea to find out what's wrong with the engine.

You can make starting easier on damp mornings by wrapping the engine in a blanket after stopping it the night before, to keep it dry and cosy. But remember: **REMOVE THE BLANKET BEFORE STARTING THE ENGINE!** I know someone whose car caught fire because he forgot.

When the engine is running smoothly, release the accelerator so that it just ticks over. Once you start driving, the oil and ignition lights should go out. If not, stop and get the car checked. The ignition light means the battery is running down.

Keep it dry and cosy

BEAR IN MIND

- *Accelerator and choke use varies*
- *No acclerator with automatic choke*
- *Work choke back in once driving*
- *Trying too long floods the engine*
- *Trying too long flattens the battery*
- *Stop if oil light stays on*
- *Stop if ignition light stays on once driving*

Starting with a flat battery

1. JUMP START

With ignition off, use jump leads to connect the battery in your car to the battery of a second car, positive to positive and negative to negative.

Cars must not be touching. Start the second car's engine, then start your car normally.

2. BUMP START

Select top gear. With ignition on, hold down the clutch as other people push the car to build up speed.

Release the clutch so the momentum turns the engine. Try again, and again.

PROCEDURE

- Cockpit drill
- Check handbrake is on
- Check gear is in neutral
- Choke if necessary
- Turn ignition on
- Push down accelerator slightly

- Operate starter
- Release starter when engine fires
- Ease off accelerator
- Push choke in a bit
- If the engine won't fire, rest a moment

MOVING OFF

This is the first crucial manoeuvre to learn. Below is the procedure for moving off straight on the level. See page 9 for hills and angles. First do your cockpit drill and start the engine.

Push down the clutch and move the gear lever to first. If the lever won't go in, release and re-apply the clutch and try again. If that fails, try holding the clutch down while moving the lever to the second gear position and then straight to first.

The engine has been ticking over, but now you push the accelerator a little to speed it to an even hum. Let the clutch up smoothly until the engine note changes. This is the biting point, where the engine is on the point of moving the wheels. Hold the pedals there while you look in the mirrors for a big enough gap (where other vehicles won't have to swerve, slow down or crash for you). When you see one, glance over your right shoulder to check your blind spot, where your view in the mirrors is blocked. Watch for pedestrians. If safe, indicate right (if there are any drivers or pedestrians around to see the signal). Pull the handbrake a little and push in the button, so you are holding the lever up with your hand.

When you are sure it is safe to go, look in the mirrors and over your right shoulder again, bring the clutch up a little more, releasing the handbrake smoothly as you feel the engine nudging the car forwards. Pull away from the kerb, pressing the accelerator further and easing the clutch right up.

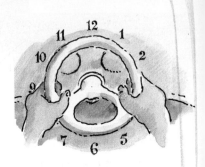

Hold the wheel at ten to two or quarter to three

BITING POINT

The engine is linked to the gearbox via two plates held together by springs. It drives one which turns the other by friction. Pushing the clutch separates these plates. If your foot rests on the pedal while driving, they slip slightly, wearing out faster and making the car slower. But if you need to go very slowly you slip the plates on purpose.

The point at which they are just brushing, almost apart but not quite, should have been the kissing point, but in this unromantic world it's called the biting point instead.

Look over your right shoulder again

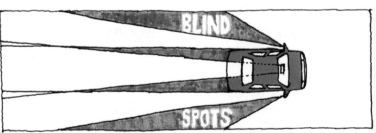

Even correctly adjusted mirrors don't show everything

BEAR IN MIND

- *Need big enough gap so that others do not need to swerve or slow*
- *Watch for pedestrians and bikes*
- *Need more acceleration uphill*
- *Need foot-brake downhill*
- *Need bigger gap on any hill*
- *Look especially carefully when moving off at an angle*

Starting on hills and angles

UP HILL Moving off uphill is sometimes specifically tested; you must not move back at all.

The procedure is the same as for starting the car on the level, but you must remember to use more acceleration. Reaching the biting point may also mean lifting the clutch further. You must wait for a larger gap than normal in traffic because you will need longer to get up to speed.

DOWN HILL

Easier than moving off uphill, but you must prevent the car from rolling forward, using the foot-brake.

After engaging the gear (usually second) push the foot-brake instead of the accelerator. Look for a safe gap and signal in the usual way. Then smoothly release the foot-brake and clutch when you want to move. Again, wait for a large gap, this time because approaching traffic will take longer to slow down if you misjudge it.

AT AN ANGLE

You must look around with extra care because you will be swinging out wide into the road. Be ready for anyone who steps out from between parked vehicles or opens a car door without looking. If space is limited, be careful not to swing into an oncoming driver's path.

Give yourself time to move out very slowly, keeping the clutch just above biting point, so that you can complete all the steering. Remember, you must not turn the wheel while you are stationary.

PROCEDURE

- Do cockpit drill
- Start engine
- Push down clutch
- Select first gear
- Push accelerator a little
- Lift clutch to biting point
- Look in mirrors for gap
- Look over right shoulder
- Signal if necessary
- Get ready to release handbrake
- Look to check it is still safe
- Ease off clutch
- Ease off brake as engine bites
- Release handbrake
- Pull away from kerb
- Ease clutch right off
- Accelerate
- Check position, mirror, speed

NORMAL STOPPING

Better to brake gently for a long time

Don't wait until you are moving before you start wondering how to stop. It's easier than moving off but it's still a manoeuvre you must practise, so find a safe place to stop where you won't endanger or inconvenience others. For instance, don't pull up where someone may come round a bend and see you too late to avoid hitting you, or where you would be blocking an opening or the road itself. Use your mirrors and decide whether to signal. If there is anyone to tell, signal left. Be careful if there is an opening on the left; someone may think you are turning. Pass it before indicating, or make it clear by your position near the kerb and your slow speed that you are stopping well before it. Move in if you are pulling up at the side of the road, stopping about 10–20 cm from the kerb. You can stop in any gear. There's no need to change down, though where you may not have to stop, such as at a junction, drop to second before you arrive so that you can pull away again.

Ease right off the accelerator and press the brake lightly to give a signal to those following, then progressively more firmly. It's better to brake gently for a long time rather than hard and fast. This saves fuel and lets others adjust to what you're doing. Hard braking also throws the weight of the car and passengers forwards, making steering more difficult. Very hard braking will lock the wheels and the car will skid; don't do it. When you're about to stop (below 10 to 15 mph, depending on the car) press the clutch to prevent stalling. Don't press it before then: you are not supposed to coast with the wheels disconnected from the engine. If the gear lever quivers and the engine coughs, you have left the clutch a bit late. Unless you're on a slope, ease off the brake as you stop. Put the handbrake on by pushing the button, pulling the lever and then releasing the button. Just pulling the lever wears out the ratchet. Unless the foot-brake fails, or you want to skid the back of your car round like they do in TV cop shows, never use your handbrake while moving.

SECURITY

Usually, keep doors unlocked while driving so you're less likely to be trapped in a crash. But in town, where people drive slowly and often stop, or if you feel at risk, keeping them locked against crime may be less dangerous. When you park, secure doors and windows. Leaving animals, such as dogs, in a car is a criminal offence. Don't leave valuables or things that look like they may contain them (such as coats) on show. Cover the radio, or get a coded one. Don't leave car documents in the car. Fit security devices (such as an alarm). Etch

Park near a light

the registration number on the windows. If you'll be leaving or returning to the car at night, park near a light.

PROCEDURE

- Use mirrors
- Signal if necessary
- Ease completely off accelerator
- Brake lightly
- Brake progressively harder
- Just before stopping, push clutch down

- Ease off foot-brake as you stop
- Handbrake on
- Gear to neutral
- Feet off pedals

MSM ROUTINE

MIRROR, SIGNAL, MANOEUVRE. Before any change of position or speed, you must look in your mirror. If there is anyone who might find it useful you must give a signal. If (for instance) a driver is coming up in an overtaking position, or a bike is slipping through where a car cannot go,

then give the signal early and look again to see their reaction. If they keep coming you may have to wait before manoeuvring.

The manoeuvre should start with PSL: get into the correct POSITION, make sure you're at the right SPEED, LOOK and act on what you see.

If a bike is slipping through…

BEAR IN MIND

- *Use signals to clarify your position but don't signal where it might confuse people*
- *Don't change down*
- *Leave space for gentle braking*
- *Never stop where it will endanger or inconvenience others*

DRIVING ALONG

Just going along may seem easy enough, but the road ahead will not always be straight and empty. There will be curves, hills, obstructions, even people doing silly things (you won't be one, of course). Expect the unexpected. Be alert. Watch and read the road ahead and in your mirrors. Watch for and understand road signs.

These will warn you of hazards ahead but they cannot tell you how other road users will act. If you see problems early, you can slow down and manoeuvre in good time to avoid them. If you observe and signal properly, you won't become a problem yourself.

Expect the unexpected

Road position

In general, keep left. On a normal two-way road, depending on its width, you drive just to the left of the centre of your lane, often about 1–2 metres from the kerb. Do not go too close to the centre, where you may hit a car coming in the other direction. (If you are both doing 30 mph, then a head-on crash is like hitting a wall at 60.) Don't go too close to the edge where drains and other bumps will jerk your steering and your

passengers and where you may hit the kerb and damage a tyre. (This may cause a dangerous blow-out later.)

In a road divided into lanes, keep to the centre of your lane. Use the left-hand lane where possible. When you overtake or want to turn right, use the right-hand lane on your half of the road. Don't cross to the other half unless signs and markings allow, and you're sure it's safe.

Speed

Obviously you must keep within the speed limit, but going too slowly (unless conditions dictate) will annoy other drivers and make you fail the test. You may sometimes meet a '38 mph driver' who sits in front of you doing 38 when the limit is 60, and then pulls away when it's 30 because he's still doing 38. It's even more irritating being followed the other way by one of these. He sits on your tail in the 30 mph zone, overtakes when the limit rises and sits in front of you at 38. It may take great self-control, but just because he is not reacting to road conditions doesn't mean you can forget how to drive well. Remember that the speed

limit may not always be safe. You should be able to stop within the distance you can see, so if visibility is restricted (by fog, trees, a plague of locusts) or if the road surface would make it harder to stop (rain, snow), slow down. Also go slow where there are hazards to negotiate.

There are places with a 20 mph limit, but most suburban side roads still allow 30, despite being full of parked cars, playing children, dogs, cats and so on. Whatever the signs say, you should consider the conditions of each road individually and assess the potential for hazards, adjusting your speed accordingly.

Hills

Steep hills pose particular problems. You need more brake and less accelerator going down and the opposite going up. In either case you may need a lower gear, for power going up and for control going down. Engine braking, when you slow by easing off the accelerator, will not work as well in a high gear going downhill. Don't rely on brakes alone to control speed. Most cars have drum brakes, which are less effective when hot. Change to a lower gear before reaching the hill, especially a down hill where using the clutch may make you go faster. Leave a long gap: going up hill, the car in front can stop quickly; going down hill, you can't stop quickly.

Avoid overtaking on hills. Heavy vehicles may slow to a crawl going uphill, but if you overtake, you'll be facing downhill traffic that will have trouble stopping if you misjudge the space.

Change to lower gear before reaching the hill

Bends

As you steer, feed the wheel through your hands. Don't allow it to slip back and don't cross your hands. Most drivers do both, but they shouldn't and if you want to pass your test you mustn't.

There are two problems with bends. First: you will be thrown outwards. If the road is slanted inwards this is eased, but since it has camber (it's dome-shaped) for drainage, most right-hand bends will tip you the wrong way. On a left-hand bend the camber helps, but the curve is sharper. Slow down before the bend: changing gear on the bend means steering with one hand; and braking on the bend throws the weight of the car on to the front outside wheel, which may cause a skid. A little braking on the approach will give you time to assess the bend. Go round the curve with enough acceleration for steady speed. Many bends are 'spiral' (sharper towards the middle), so pick your speed with care. Take a 'Double Bend' road sign as a warning to prepare early for the change of direction.

Second: you may not be able to see as well. The curve could hide obstructions, openings, horses, llamas, UFOs … For the best vision, keep well to the left on right-hand bends. On left-hand bends, keep to the middle of your lane. You could see more from nearer the centre of the road, but drivers coming the other way may cut the corner and you would pass too close.

SLOWING

If you ease off the accelerator, the engine will slow the car, unless you are going downhill, but you generally need the foot-brake for a large reduction in speed. Slow gradually and smoothly. Use your mirror, and signal by braking very lightly to operate the brake light. Brake progressively harder, but never too hard, unless you want to stop. If you don't intend to stop, you will probably need to change down through the gears, keeping to ones appropriate for your speed, so that you can drive on or accelerate.

You should

1. *Anticipate*

2. *Know your car's limitations and your own*

3. *Note different road conditions*

4. *Give yourself time to brake progressively*

5. *Avoid skids rather than trying to control them (see 'Skids' page 60).*

13

CHANGING GEAR

To keep the engine speed within its narrow, efficient range while changing road speed, you need the gears. Know the gear positions so you can change without looking down. You may need a light sideways pressure on the lever while in neutral to find, for instance, first rather than third, and a hard push or lift for reverse. You move off in first or second and change up through the gears as you speed up, easing off the accelerator each time because the engine needs to turn less for the same road speed in the higher gears. Slowing down, you brake and then, if you are not stopping, change down to the appropriate gear for the new speed. You do not need to go through each gear in turn when changing down: just pick the right one.

Also, the engine delivers more power and control in the faster part of its range, so if you will soon need this (such as when approaching a hill, a curve or when about to overtake), change down. You should be in the correct gear before you start the manoeuvre. Changes should be smooth. Don't force the lever. Modern cars have synchromesh, allowing changes over a wide range of engine and road speeds. Which gear you need for which speed depends on the car and conditions, but as a rough average guide to get you started: first is for 0–10 mph, second is for 0–20, or up to 30 if you need more power, third is for 10–30 or up to 70 if you need more power, fourth is for 20 upwards, and fifth is for 30 upwards. In general, a more powerful car will need fewer gear changes.

SOME GEAR PROBLEMS

If you find that the engine revs rise rapidly during the gear change or the car doesn't pull following a gear change, it's likely that either the clutch pedal has gone down before the accelerator is raised enough, or you've gone back on the gas too early, before the clutch pedal is fully raised.

PROCEDURE FOR CHANGING

UP

- Left hand on gear lever
- Push clutch right down and ease off accelerator (but don't remove your foot from it)
- Move lever to next highest gear
- Let clutch right up smoothly while gradually pressing accelerator

DOWN

- Left hand on gear lever
- Press clutch right down while keeping a little pressure on either the accelerator (to raise engine speed for a smooth change) or the footbrake (to prevent road speed from rising), depending on conditions
- Move lever to correct gear for new lower speed
- Let clutch up
- Accelerate or brake as necessary

Four-wheel drive

A few cars have permanent four-wheel drive and some others allow you to select it with an extra lever. On the road you get better cornering and road-holding. You can also handle the mud and bumps of off-road driving, where you can play explorers and get stuck. A saloon will not have a big enough gap between the ground and the bottom of the car for really hard terrain. Vehicles designed for rough country do.

This makes them higher and, in theory, slightly more likely to tip over on a tight bend, though in fact this is unlikely to happen. Using four-wheel drive on the road requires no special skills, but going across country is a book in itself. It is not enough to get tough, wear a bandanna and say 'Yo!'. Before bravely trying any difficult expeditions, attend an off-the-road driving course.

Using automatic gears

An automatic gearbox selects the gear for you based on engine load and speed. This gives you more time to worry about other things, but there are special rules. There's a gear selector, but no clutch. Use your right foot for both accelerator and brake, except during manoeuvres when you can have a foot on each pedal. Only use 'Park' (P) when stationary. Start the engine in P or 'Neutral' (N) and go to 'Drive' (D) when you want to move. Engine braking doesn't work as well because the car selects a higher gear as the load drops. So going downhill, for example, select 3,

2 or 1, which keeps the car in that gear. Always use the handbrake when stationary. Unless you are in P or N, any accelerator pressure causes movement. Just the engine ticking over may make you 'creep' forwards. Avoid any heavy acceleration (especially during manoeuvres) unless you want the 'kick-down' for a burst of power, when you press the accelerator hard down to get a lower gear. On corners, slow as you approach and use slight acceleration on the turn to stop the gear changing up.

A pass in an automatic car only lets you drive automatics, but a pass with manual gears lets you drive either type.

OVERTAKING

Overtaking a moving vehicle is the most dangerous manoeuvre to get wrong, so patiently following the car in front is often a better tactic. However, on the test you would be expected to overtake slow vehicles, such as milk floats, to avoid holding up traffic.

Imagine passing someone doing 20 mph at the speed limit of 30. While you creep by at your extra 10 mph, you may hit an oncoming car at a combined speed of 60. So pick a place where you can see a long way ahead. Don't overtake where an oncoming car may be hidden by a bend, a hill, a bridge, a dip in the road, fog, the vehicle in front or anything else. Don't overtake at pedestrian or level crossings or where you would stray across double white lines with a solid one your side, or after a 'No Overtaking' sign (surprise). The main difference between overtaking where you mustn't and overtaking where you shouldn't, is the even higher chance of an accident. Don't overtake when it's pointless, such as when you are about to turn off.

Don't just follow the car in front around something you are both overtaking, but do your own thinking (you'd do your own crashing). Remember, a heavy vehicle may crawl uphill but speed down. Try to avoid overtaking on steep hills, but if you can't, wait for an even bigger gap. Bikes, motorbikes and horses may wobble so give them lots of room as you pass. Where opposing traffic lanes are separated by a common overtaking lane, do not pull out into the path of an oncoming car also pulling out. On dual carriageways, look in your mirror for fast cars coming up in the lane you're entering.

Don't cross double white lines

Use your mirrors. Check in the offside (driver's side) door mirror to see if anyone is overtaking you. If they are, let them pass first. (Slow down to help them.) Position yourself near enough to the vehicle in front to pass smoothly, but far enough back to see past it. For fast acceleration you may need a lower gear. Consider hazards, conditions, the speed and position of oncoming vehicles, and what the driver ahead may do. If there is a bike in front, he may swing out to overtake it while you are overtaking him. Mirror again and always signal right. Check forward and behind again. Begin to close the gap between you and the other vehicle but not so close that you can't abort the manoeuvre successfully. Pull out in a smooth line and overtake quickly. Move back when your mirrors (the nearside door mirror and your interior mirror) show you are clear of the passed vehicle and any others that may have been hidden by it. Relying only on your nearside door mirror as guidance will often cause you to cut in too early when moving back to your own side as the image shown makes the passed vehicle seem further away than it really is.

PROCEDURE

- See a long way ahead and behind in your mirror
- Consider changing to a lower gear
- Mirror
- Signal right
- Check forward and behind again
- Begin to close the gap
- Pull out smoothly
- Pass quickly
- Move in as soon as it's safe

PASSING ON THE LEFT

You must not pass on the left, except when

1. the vehicle in front is signalling right and you can get by on the left, but watch for oncoming cars turning across your bows into an opening on your left and go slowly and carefully if space is limited
2. you're in the lane for your left turn
3. traffic is moving slowly in queues and the queue on your right is slower, but don't change lanes to overtake on the left
4. you're on a one-way street (but not a dual carriageway).

Passing obstructions

With moving vehicles you have a choice, but stationary obstructions either have to be passed or you must stay where you are, looking pathetic. It may be a parked car, road works or anything else. Road works may have their own traffic lights, or a man holding a 'Stop/Go' sign, but otherwise:

Act early. Use your mirrors. If you need to use the other half of the road, look for a good gap. Adjust your speed so that you can move out and back in a smooth line, rather than getting close and steering hard. If you must wait, stay well back so you can see and still take a smooth line. Don't just follow the person in front around an obstruction. The gap may not be big enough. Make your own decision.

Only signal (briefly) if you must (for instance if you must steer hard or to warn those behind of what's coming up) and if it will not confuse.

Do not weave in and out of a row of parked cars, but take a smooth line. Cars on the clear side of the road have priority, so pull in for them. If your side is clear but it's easier for you to stop, then be courteous and let the other driver go first, or if there's room for two lines of traffic, stay close to the kerb to give the others room.

Make sure the cars you are about to pass are parked, and not just waiting at a pedestrian crossing or something. Look ahead for traffic lights or beacons. Be very careful if there is anyone in the driver's seat of a stationary car: it may be about to move off. Leave a gap in case someone opens a door and if there is too little room, slow down. Watch for pedestrians stepping out from between parked vehicles.

- *You need a very long gap*
- *Don't overtake unless you have to*
- *Give bikes, motorbikes and horses lots of room*
- *Don't just follow the overtaking car in front round*
- *There is extra danger on hills*

EMERGENCY STOP

If you observe and act properly you should never need the emergency stop.' Being clairvoyant helps too. The unpredictable happens and you must be ready. That's why, near the start of the test, you will be asked to pull over and will be told that when the examiner taps the dashboard, you must stop as if a child has run into the road.

For the emergency stop only, don't use your mirrors. (You should know what's there anyway and on the test the examiner will have checked.) If someone *is* too close, metal cars can take an impact better than a child's flesh and bones. Don't signal – no time for any MSMing! To keep control, hold the wheel tightly with both hands.

There is a danger of skidding. Brake progressively, like a normal stop but much quicker. The brake's friction should be just less than the tyre's friction with the road. If the wheel slows too fast, so the tyre loses grip, it will lock and start to

Sliding wheels have less road-holding

skid. Sliding wheels have less road-holding and less direction than rolling wheels, so you will actually slow more slowly, lose steering, scream, swear and fail. In the advanced anti-skid technique of cadence braking (not required for the test), you brake, then release it just before the wheels lock, brake again, etc. Some cars have wonderful anti-lock brakes which do something like this automatically and let you steer while braking hard, but learners should get the progressive braking habit anyway. Remember, you can't brake as hard in slippery conditions like rain. Don't press the clutch until you are about to stop, so you get engine braking too. ONLY once you've stopped, apply the handbrake and select neutral. Before you move off again, remember you are out in the road so look over your shoulders at the blind spots on both sides.

18

PROCEDURE

- Brake as hard as you can without locking the wheels
- When about to stop, press clutch
- Keep both hands on the wheel until you've stopped
- Once stationary, apply handbrake
- Select neutral
- Look round both sides before moving off again

ANTICIPATION

Much of driving is anticipation: you see a corner and prepare to turn; you see a car coming and wait. But most people don't see all they could.

Look under cars and through windows to see what's behind them. Be ready for pedestrians (especially children, who are unpredictable and are harder to see) coming from behind an ice-cream van or bus. Look for gaps in the trees where you can get an idea of traffic crossing your path. On bends, look for traffic reflected in windows.

Watch others' behaviour. Their speed and position may show what they mean to do. If oncoming cars have lights on in daylight, there may

Look under cars

be fog ahead. Someone who stops at a green light and goes on red may be tired or upset, so give them room. Pedestrians may act carelessly in the rain. Children and animals may dart out into the road without looking.

There are thousands more possible examples. Use your eyes and experience and act on what you see.

Stopping distances

For your test you must learn the stopping distances in the Highway Code. But they are not easy to remember, and many people find it hard to judge distances anyway. You can learn to judge them by counting your paces to objects you see ahead while walking. A rough rule for the distances, though no substitute for knowing them for the test, is a metre for every mile per hour (in good conditions and a reasonably new car). In bad conditions double this. Thinking distance is about one-third of the stopping distance. Choose your speed so that you can stop within the distance you can see and also leave a gap of this length to the car in front (difficult below 30 or 40 mph, but at least leave your thinking distance).

Another easy-to-remember rule of

ONE, TWO...

thumb is: leave a two-second gap between you and the car in front. Do this by watching it pass a marker such as a lamp-post and then saying 'Only a fool breaks the two second rule'. When you finish you shouldn't have passed the marker. In bad conditions say it twice.

If the driver behind you is too close, increase the gap in front, so that if something happens up ahead you have time to react gently and the person on your tail has more time to react to what you're doing.

PARKING

If you can, you should always park off the road. If you must park on the road then you must not cause danger to anyone. For instance, don't park on a bend where a driver may see you too late to avoid you or where you may block the view of other road users. You must not cause an obstruction to traffic – if the blocked traffic includes an emergency vehicle then your bad parking may cost a life. In a narrow road you may not be able to park at all, or at least not opposite another parked car. Some people ease traffic flow by parking with two wheels on the pavement, but unless there's a sign telling you to do this, don't, it's illegal: a blind person may walk into the car or you may leave too small a gap for prams and wheelchairs to pass. Don't block a junction or opening. Just because other drivers are badly parked doesn't mean you should follow their example.

There are many places where you must not park. You will find a list in the Highway Code but a general rule is that unusual road markings such as red, yellow or zig-zag lines at the edge of the road, or double white lines down its centre, are bad news.

Two wheels on the pavement is illegal

Yellow lines normally accompany a small plate showing the times that you may not park: the more paint on the road, the more times. You can usually load and unload, but closing the boot between trips to fetch and carry may make your loading into parking and you will be in trouble. Beware: these parking restrictions apply even if you are off the carriageway, the other side of the lines. Don't park in a lane meant for something else, such as buses or bikes. You would not want someone leaving their bike blocking your road would you? There are places without lines that still have restrictions, such as where a residents' parking scheme is in operation. There will still be signs, but they may be down the road and round the corner. There is no good rule here, but if all the other cars in the road have funny-looking stickers in their windows then you may be better off elsewhere.

Don't park after a 'Clearway' sign, or on a motorway except on the hard shoulder in an emergency. (So don't use the hard shoulder to cry on.)

Don't park after a clearway sign

PARKING ON HILLS

There is always the danger, when parked on hills, of the brake failing and the car going off for a journey on its own. To prevent this, leave it in gear: first gear when facing uphill, or reverse when facing down. Leave an automatic in Park. Make sure your handbrake is on firmly. Also, leave the wheels turned so that if the vehicle starts to move it will be stopped by the kerb or will roll off the road. For this, point the wheels towards the kerb or edge of road when facing downhill. Facing uphill: turn the wheels away from the kerb only when you can park very close to it; where you can't or where there is no kerb, turn the wheels towards the edge. Parking on a hill is more difficult so leave a bigger gap.

Turn the wheels to prevent the car rolling

Parking at night or in fog

When you park at night you should be facing in the direction of traffic flow so that your reflectors are pointed the right way and, unless you are in a road with a speed limit of 30 or less and are more than 10 metres from any junction, you must leave your sidelights on.

In fog, again, you need your lights although people often do not bother in residential streets. Don't let this fool you into thinking that you can leave your car safely on a faster road. Get off the road if you can, and if you absolutely can't, then leave the sidelights on. Don't use your hazard warning lights as an excuse to park where you like. They are only for emergencies such as breakdowns. You must not leave your headlights on when parked because they may dazzle others and make them think the aliens are landing. This could be distracting.

Facing the direction of the traffic flow

SIGNALS

The main way you communicate your intentions to others is by position and speed. However, an early warning lets people adjust earlier and more safely, so you use signals. Obviously you want your meaning to be clear, so use them with care: when slowing, use light early braking to show following drivers your brake light; when turning, leave your turn signal until you've passed the opening before the one you want. If you intend to stop just after a turning, don't signal left until you've passed it: your brake light and position near the kerb will indicate that something's happening. Hazard warning lights are for breakdowns (stop them before moving off) or when you must slow quickly on a dual carriageway due to a hazard ahead (only use them briefly).

Understand other people's signals. Flashing blue lights, maybe with sirens, mean 'Emergency – get out of the way quickly but safely'; flashing green means 'Doctor – give way'; flashing amber means 'Slow vehicle – be careful'. When a bus signals it wants to join the traffic you should let it in if it is safe to do so, even though you'll be stuck behind it. People may give signals which the Highway Code says they shouldn't use. Interpret unofficial signals by other drivers with great care. Be aware that not everyone is careful: don't bet your life on a signal meaning what it should.

HEADLIGHT FLASHER

On the test you MUST follow the Highway Code rule that the headlight flasher should, like the horn, only be used to warn of your presence. Be careful: some people use it incorrectly.

In the real world, people often use the flasher for general communication. I don't mean they tap away on it in Morse code. It's more like a grunt; its meaning depends on the situation. For example, in a narrow road, you meet another car. You have priority, but you see he has less room so you stop and flash to invite him to go first. He proceeds (slowly) and flashes as he passes to say thanks. Both flashes have clear meanings because of their context and you're both going slowly, so if there's a misunderstanding you have time to act. Had you waited without flashing, you may have fallen asleep for all he knew.

But take care: perhaps the other vehicle isn't flashing you. It may just have its headlights on, even during the day (especially if it's a motorbike) or may be flashing someone else, or the person inviting you to proceed may not have seen all the possible hazards you face.

If you obey the Highway Code's rule that flashes are just to warn, be aware that not everyone will use them only in that way, and not everyone will assume that is what you mean by the signal.

Although all but the first of these are unofficial, flashers are often assumed to: warn of your presence (especially when you're not allowed to use your horn); to invite someone to proceed even though you have priority; to say 'Thanks'; to tell the person in front, in the overtaking lane of a dual carriage-way or motorway, to move over (Don't do this – if it's done to you, only move back to the left if you won't be cutting in); to invite a car in the lane on the right back to the left, into a gap in front of you; to tell an oncoming car to dip its headlights (you should slow down or stop if dazzled); to warn speeding cars of a police speed trap (this is ILLEGAL); to give a warning (for example, to oncoming cars who'll meet danger ahead).

HORN

If a flash is like a grunt, then a honk on the horn is like a scream. Its only use is to warn someone you are there. Keep to this.

Even using the horn to warn needs care. You mustn't use it in town between 11.30 p.m. and 7 a.m. so you won't wake people up. You must not honk if stationary, unless there's danger from a moving vehicle, so no hooting to tell friends you've arrived outside their house. It's considered good practice to hoot before overtaking or at sharp bends in narrow minor roads where vision is bad, though a headlight flash (where it could be seen) may be less annoying. Be ready to hoot where there are a lot of pedestrians who may jump out. Generally, if you anticipate properly, you rarely need your horn. If you're always honking then either you have no luck, no skill, or no manners.

HAND SIGNALS

The Highway Code describes various hand signals, and circumstances where they're to be used. Learn them and how to use them correctly. In practice though, you'd only use them when signalling to people directing traffic; when your indicator lights aren't working; or when you're the leading car stopping at a zebra crossing. You're only likely to use them rarely. Remember that you need both hands to steer while manoeuvring, rather than using one to wind down the window and signal. Even on the test, you shouldn't give the slowing signal if time is short or if you may have to steer. It's more important that you know how and when to use them, should the need arise.

At a zebra crossing, the Highway Code says you should signal because the person waiting to cross can't see your brake-lights. They can, however, see that you're slowing down. The right-turn arm signal can make things clearer if you pass a parked car just before the point where you intend to turn right and you should consider it if it leaves the car behind in no doubt as to your intentions. However, if you drive slowly enough to switch the indicators off for a moment after the overtake, then back on to show there's another manoeuvre to come, this may work just as well.

Another reason for not using hand signals is, unfortunately, crime. Especially if you've stopped, a mugger, or an angry motorist (it happens) may attack you through the open window, probably grabbing that signalling hand.

Never drive with your arm out of the window: people may think you're signalling and get confused. Know and always obey signals from police or traffic wardens.

SIGNS AND MARKINGS

Even though you've never seen this sign before

Ａs you drive you're bombarded with information and commands by signs. Read the Highway Code and learn them. They mainly use a standard European system which makes most of them self-explanatory. This is good, because although you must learn the ones in the Highway Code for the test, there are others so obscure you may never encounter them. Having a system means that when you see, for instance, a silhouette of a horse and cart in a red circle, you can recognise it as 'No Horse-drawn Vehicles' even though you've never seen this sign before. There are a few exceptions to the rules that you must learn separately, from your Highway Code.

Road signs are placed for your own safety and that of other road users. It is important that you understand their meanings and how to react to the information they convey.

Road markings often back-up signs. They are supposed to be visible when the signs may be obscured by traffic, though in fact it's usually the other way round, with the lane arrows that you need to see covered by stationary vehicles. It's important, therefore, to spot any direction signs on the approach to a junction. Other road markings convey a message all on their own. These may say something about the bit of road they are on, such as double white lines where you must not overtake or stop; may direct you, such as lane arrows; or may give a message with a symbol or words, such as 'Keep Clear' (really reading the road). Generally, the more paint, the more important the message. Beware: road markings can become almost invisible in bad weather.

Road markings

Unlike signs, there's no simple system for markings, but there are things to bear in mind. The direction arrow on a lane indicates where it goes, not the exact place where you turn. Sometimes, curved arrows remind you to move left; going in the other direction over these, you may feel you're driving the wrong way, but try not to panic. It's often a bad idea to park on anything yellow! In the case of box junctions, you may not enter the box unless your exit is clear so that you are not forced to stop in the area marked by the box, although a queue of cars turning right can wait on the yellow for oncoming traffic to pass, provided their exit is clear. Yellow lines across the lane are to remind you to slow down either after a fast road or on the approach to a hazard such as a roundabout. Think twice before crossing a solid white line. Where these surround hatching, you may not enter the marked area, though you can if the lines are broken. The short broken lines at the road centre become long where there is danger, such as a hill.

Types of sign

Usually round. If they stop you doing something, they normally have black symbols on a white background in a red border (e.g. 'Maximum Speed').

If they demand that you do something, they're usually white on blue with a white border (e.g. 'Minimum Speed', 'Ahead Only').

A diagonal red line through something means 'NOT' (e.g. 'End of Minimum Speed', 'No Right Turn').

Some signs are qualified by plates. Exceptions to the above include 'No Entry' (red background), 'Stop' (octagonal), 'Give Way' (upside-down triangle), 'One-way' and bus lane signs (rectangular), 'Stop – Children' (yellow background), 'National Speed Limit' (white with no border).

In a road with lamp-posts the usual speed limit is 30 mph. If the limit is 40 or 50, or the national limit for that type of road (usually 60 mph) applies, small versions of these signs will appear along it.

Usually black symbols on white in a red triangle. If there's no symbol for the hazard, it will be worded in the triangle or on a plate. Signs meaning 'School' may have amber lights which flash when the crossing patrol is there.

Where there's a diagram of a junction, the thick line has priority.

Exceptions include 'Distance to Stop/Give Way Line' (inverted empty triangle), 'Sharp Deviation' (chevrons on black rectangle), 'Level Crossing Without Barrier' (red diagonal cross).

Rectangles or pointed rectangles. Direction signs are white in a black border when local or on non-primary routes, green in white on primaries and blue in white on motorways.

Some local information and signs for pedestrians or cyclists (e.g. 'Hospital', 'Library', 'No Through Road') also use blue in a white border. A junction of important roads normally has three signs: one well before it, one at the junction itself and one just after it to tell you where you went wrong.
Tourist information signs are brown, and temporary signs such as diversions and contraflows tend to be yellow.

When diverted off a motorway, you will often be shown a symbol to look out for and follow to get you back on course.

TURNING LEFT INTO SIDE-ROAD

You can't just keep going along the same road. At some point, you'll want to turn at a junction. The easiest is a left turn off a major road, because you have priority over the other cars. However, there's still a procedure to be followed and points to watch.

Well back from your turning (around 200 metres) look in the mirror and, if safe, signal left and start to slow gently. Position yourself about a metre from the kerb. As you slow, take third gear and then second, remembering that pressing the clutch may make you go faster downhill. Try to finish braking before you start the turn. As you get close, check for pedestrians crossing the side-road and give way to them. Check for bikes overtaking between you and the kerb as you slow and they catch you up. Never overtake just before turning. If you must cross a bus or cycle lane r a tramway, check both ways for traffic first. Make the turn at walking pace.

Don't cut the corner and mount the kerb, or go so fast you swing to the wrong side of the minor road. Once on the new road, check your mirrors,

make sure your indicators have cancelled and speed up if safe.

If there's another turning just before yours, don't signal until you've passed it. If this means slowing before you indicate left, use gentle braking to show following drivers your brake-lights. If the driver in front is also indicating left, don't get too close: he may intend to stop before the turning and you'll need room to pass. Don't rush blindly into a side-road with limited visibility. There may be a parked car, or the road may be full of traffic. Also, watch for cars parked on the other side of the minor road, which may force drivers on to the wrong side, on a collision course with you as you enter.

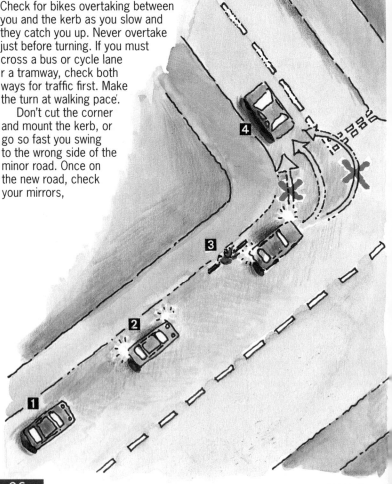

One-way streets

In one-way streets, traffic will all be going the same way (surprise) and usually in several lanes. Remember that it may be going faster than in two-way streets and also that people can overtake on your left as well as on your right.

In general, use the left-hand lane if you intend to turn left and right for right. If you are going ahead and there's no centre lane, be guided by signs and markings. Normally, when you are going ahead, use the left of two lanes unless it has obstructions or slower traffic. Try to get in lane early. If you find yourself in the wrong lane at the junction, don't make a sudden change, but go the way your position implies and get back on course by some other route. Getting lost is better than causing a crash and it was your fault anyway.

If for any reason you do find yourself going the wrong way up a one-way street, go very slowly and carefully and stop if anyone is coming. Get going in the right direction as soon as possible, either by a U-turn or taking the first turning you come to (regardless of whether you want that direction, unless it's another one-way in the wrong direction). Going the wrong way is VERY dangerous.

Someone may emerge without looking

DRIVING PAST A JUNCTION

Even if you're on the major road and you don't intend to turn, you should still treat junctions with caution. Someone may emerge without looking, or nose out too far to see what's happening. Go slowly enough to take evasive action. Be especially careful at crossroads, where someone may cross without looking. Take care passing cars waiting to turn, and don't overtake other moving vehicles. Remember that long vehicles may need the whole road to make the turn.

If you want to cross the major road and it's safe to proceed, don't go fast but use good acceleration to avoid stalling.

BEAR IN MIND

- *Observation is paramount to safety*
- *Finish braking before you turn*
- *Don't overtake just before turn*
- *Look both ways when crossing bus/cycle/tram lanes*
- *Don't cut corner or swing out*
- *Don't signal until after opening before the one you want*
- *Don't rush in blindly where you couldn't see any obstruction*

PROCEDURE

- Look in mirrors [1]
- Signal left [2]
- Start to slow
- Good observation, left and right
- Position about a metre from kerb
- Slow through third gear to second
- Check for pedestrians and bikes [3]
- Turn at walking pace [4]
- Look in mirrors
- Check indicators have cancelled
- Speed up

TURNING RIGHT INTO SIDE-ROAD

Turning right is tricky because you have to cross a stream of traffic. Learn the procedure rather than learning from your cra ... mistakes.

About 300–400 metres from the opening, look in your mirror and signal right. Take a position close to the centre of the road (but not over the line) and slow down through third gear to second. You probably won't need first, unless you drop below 5 mph, you are turning up a hill, or you have to stop. You should have finished braking by the turn. As you near it, look to see if anyone is overtaking a car coming the other way and leave them room if they are. Look for a good gap in the oncoming traffic. If you time it right you may get round without stopping, which makes stalling across the other lane less likely, but you must leave yourself the option of stopping. Look for pedestrians crossing the side-road and give way to them. Before you turn you should check in the mirror for people overtaking you and, if you can, glance over your right shoulder too. If you have to stop, your front

bumper should be in line with the centre of the side-road and you should still be close to the middle of the main road, so people can pass on your left. Even if the road's too narrow for a car to pass, bikes, horses and unicycles may still be able to. Also, your position will show what you intend to do. Even if you don't need to stop, take the same course, starting your turn at this point. If you will only have to wait briefly, go into first gear and hold the clutch down ready, but otherwise you should use the handbrake and neutral. Keep your wheels straight while waiting, so that if someone hits you from behind you won't be pushed across the other lane.

When you have a big enough gap, look over your right shoulder and turn into the side-road at fast walking pace, keeping well to the left. Check mirrors and indicators. Speed up if safe. If someone stops to let you turn in front of them, watch for bikes passing them on their left.

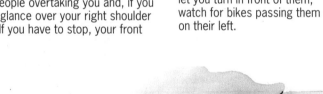

PROCEDURE

- Look in mirrors [1]
- Signal right [2]
- Move to left of road centre [3]
- Slow through third to second gear [4]
- Look for gap in oncoming traffic and into side-road
- If no gap, wait opposite road with your indicator signalling right [5]
- Position front of your vehicle level with centre of side road
- Look for pedestrians crossing [6]
- Check over your right shoulder
- Turn at walking pace [7]
- Look in mirrors
- Check indicators have cancelled
- Speed up

Turn offside to offside at crossroads, unless police, traffic wardens, road markings or the junction's layout indicate otherwise. Get eye contact with the other driver to see what he wants to do. Go slow enough to stop if there's a misunderstanding.

Other types of junction

Even at a simple side-road-joins-main-road T-junction, you need to be careful, but there are other types with their own problems.

JUNCTIONS ON BENDS The straight route has 'Give Way' lines while the main road goes round the bend. Beware of confused people and don't be one of them. Right turns off the main road pose visibility problems.

UNMARKED JUNCTIONS Unmarked except for the skids, and the remains of drivers who thought they had priority. Take extra care at unmarked crossroads.

Y-JUNCTIONS The curved route may have priority. Emerging drivers, confused by the shallow angle, may appear from nowhere, so be careful. When emerging, try to get square with the lines for better visibility.

CROSSROADS Even on the major road you should slow down: cars crossing your path may not stop. When two cars meet and both are turning right, they should turn offside to offside (nose to tail) for better visibility, unless there's a good reason to turn nearside to nearside.

STAGGERED JUNCTIONS Crossing the major road, you may have to make turns both ways in quick succession, or treat it like a crossroads, depending on the layout. Look for good gaps and remember that visibility is reduced. Avoid stalling by using good acceleration.

The majority of accidents occur at junctions, which vary widely in style. Control of the car, procedure and, above all, observation will ensure safety when entering and leaving side and major roads of all kinds.

- *Look for oncoming overtakers*
- *Need big enough gap so that nobody needs to brake or swerve*
- *First gear if you must wait*
- *Neutral and handbrake if you must wait long*
- *Finish braking by turn*
- *Wait with wheels straight*
- *People can pass on your left*

Some of this is also covered in a different way in 'Turning right into main road' (see page 32).

One or two hundred metres before the junction, look in your mirror and signal left, but delay the signal until you've passed any other left turnings. Position yourself near the kerb. Slow, and go to third gear. Notice if the junction has a 'Give Way' or a 'Stop' sign. If 'Stop', stop in third and then use handbrake and neutral. If, as you get to the corner, the car at the line is signalling right, go to second gear and squeeze by on his left if there's room. You MUST stop at the line, not over it. Don't stop half a metre back: you need to see along the road you're entering and your zone of vision will improve greatly in the last metre. If you still can't see, because of parked cars etc., then after stopping, creep forward until you can. Look around to get different views, so no nasty surprises appear from behind the window frame or that leaf stuck to the glass. When you see a gap coming which is large enough for you to emerge into without affecting other traffic, get into first gear and bring the clutch to biting point. Move into the gap when it arrives, turning

without swinging out.

If the sign was 'Give Way', go to second gear after third as you slow. You may see a good gap as you arrive and be able to turn without stopping. If you have to stop, then the procedure is as before, though if you won't have to stop for long you can select first gear and just hold your clutch down while waiting.

Watch for pedestrians crossing the roads in front of you and for bikes coming from the right which may be hard to see. Also watch for people overtaking cars coming from the left and so entering your side of the main road. A car coming from the right may be indicating left. If he means it you could emerge in front of him, but maybe he intends to stop after the opening, or has left his indicator going by mistake, so don't move until he starts to turn. You will see people on busy roads nudging into the traffic until they force it to let them in, or darting into a small gap, making approaching cars slow down. This should be avoided.

Once you have entered the main road, check your mirrors, make sure your indicator is off and increase your speed to that of the traffic.

BEAR IN MIND

TURNING LEFT INTO MAIN ROAD

- *If you can get past a waiting car signalling right, then do*
- *Position so you can see properly*
- *Move your head around*
- *Watch for pedestrians, bikes and overtakers*
- *Don't rely on people's signals*

Zones of vision

Your zone of vision is the area you can see from the driver's seat. Approaching a junction with a main road, buildings may stop you seeing much until you come level with the junction.

Other problems are obstructions such as parked cars, pedestrians, bends in the road etc. After stopping, you may have to creep forward until you can see, but there may still be blind areas. Look through the windows of parked cars, and at reflections in shop windows. Observe obstructions for a while to see if anything disappears behind them, or to notice if there appears to be movement. Emerge carefully and be prepared to stop. Remember, if you cannot see someone, they probably can't see you either.

When you are behind a large vehicle in a narrow road, stay back so that you can see a little of the junction past it. This will give you some information about the road ahead.

PROCEDURE

- Look in mirrors [1]
- Signal left
- Slow through third gear
- Position well to left of road [2]
- Notice 'Stop' or 'Give Way' [3]
- Stop in third gear if 'Stop'
- Stop in second if 'Give Way'
- Stop at line, though you may

- not need to at a 'Give Way' [4]
- Neutral and handbrake
- Prepare to go if you see gap [5]
- When gap arrives, make turn
- Look in mirrors
- Check indicators are off
- Speed up

31

When you are turning right into a main road, everyone has priority over you.

Two hundred metres from the junction, mirror and signal right, after you have passed any earlier junctions. Slow and go to third gear. Position yourself just left of the centre line. If the junction has a 'Stop' sign, pull up in third, pressing the clutch as you stop and using handbrake and neutral. If it has a 'Give Way' sign, go to second because you may be able to turn without stopping. If you do stop, go to first, or handbrake and neutral if you will have to wait long. You must stop behind the line, but only just behind because you need to be well forward for good visibility. If you still can't see along the main road, then stop and edge forward until you can. It can be difficult to get the balance right: you must see, but you don't want to push your nose so far out that someone hits it. You need gaps both ways that are large enough

to enter without making people slow or swerve. When good enough gaps are coming, get ready to move and go when they arrive, without cutting the turn. Keep looking both ways throughout the manoeuvre, but as you start, be looking in the direction with the worst visibility. Watch for pedestrians crossing your road or the main road, for bikes and for people overtaking on the main road. Glance over your right shoulder before moving, in case a bike is overtaking you. Don't rely on someone who is indicating a left turn into your road actually doing it. If someone on the main road is waiting to turn right into your road, they have priority over you (doesn't everyone?), so let them go. Remember that long vehicles need more room to turn.

Once you are in the new road, look in your mirrors, make sure your indicator is cancelled and increase speed to fit the new traffic.

PROCEDURE

- Mirrors and signal right [1]
- Slow through third gear
- Position near middle of road [2]
- Notice 'Stop' or 'Give Way' [3]
- Observation – look left and right
- Stop in third gear if 'Stop'
- Stop in second if 'Give Way'
- Stop at line, though you may not need to at a 'Give Way' [4]
- Neutral and handbrake
- When you see gaps, prepare to go
- Look over right shoulder
- With gaps both ways, turn [5]
- Look in mirrors
- Check indicators are off
- Speed up

Dual carriageways

Turning left where a central reservation separates traffic going opposite ways is the same as for normal roads, except there may be special lanes for speeding up and slowing.

Turning right, or crossing over, you use a gap in the central reservation. Cross each carriageway separately, waiting in the gap in between. If your car's too big for the gap, wait for spaces in the traffic both ways and cross in one go. Turning off, wait in the gap. Some gaps hav right-turn lanes. On fast roads you need bigger spaces in the traffic.

Some junctions on normal roads have an arrowed and hatched area reserved for right turners. Treat it like a central reservation.

BEAR IN MIND

- *Leave signal until after last opening before turn*
- *Need to be forward enough to see*
- *Get ready to move when you see gaps coming*
- *Watch for bikes, overtakers and pedestrians*
- *Don't rely on others' signals*
- *Long vehicles need room to turn*

TRAFFIC LIGHTS

Traffic lights make turns easy if you do as they say. I've listed the normal procedures, but as usual there are variations because people keep having ideas about how to improve traffic flow, so take care.

Always be ready to stop when approaching lights. Even if they're green and you're going straight ahead, slow down and go to third gear about 200 metres away. If you're going to turn, slow to second. Green means 'Go if the way is clear'. Only enter if your exit is clear. Sometimes a box junction emphasises this. If you're turning right but the way's blocked by oncoming traffic you can wait on the yellow grid (often until the next red light stops the oncoming traffic). Normally turn offside to offside with cars turning right from the other direction, unless told otherwise. As at any junction, you must give way to pedestrians crossing the road you're entering, and watch for cyclists sneaking up where you don't expect them.

If the lights go to amber as you approach, stop if safe, but don't skid to a halt and cause a crash. Despite what many drivers do, amber means 'Stop if safe' and NOT 'Go faster'. You MUST stop at a red. Red and amber precedes green, so you may be able to slow and avoid stopping, but you mustn't cross the line until the light is green.

Flashing amber means you can go if no-one's crossing

Approach in the lane marked with an arrow pointing the way you want to go: usually left for a left turn; right for right; left or right for straight ahead. Your direction may have more than one lane, especially going ahead. Before you move right to the going ahead lane, give a brief signal and stop it early so people don't think you're turning.

As well as the normal green light there may be green arrow (filter) lights to say you can go in that direction (if you're in the correct lane), even if the main red light's still showing. Also watch for signs attached to the lights, or placed nearby, telling you things like 'No Right Turn' or 'Turn Left' etc.

If you must stop, wait at the solid line and apply your handbrake. Either go into neutral, or select first and hold the clutch down (both are OK on the test). When you see the other road's lights changing, or its traffic stopping, or when your road's lights go to red and amber, get ready to move as soon as they turn green and the way is clear. Remember to watch for pedestrians, and bikes overtaking on your left.

At a pelican crossing, flashing amber means you can go if no one is on the crossing. You may see other red lights, such as flashing ones outside fire stations or airports. These always mean 'Stop'.

Watch for bikes overtaking on your left

PROCEDURE FOR GOING STRAIGHT ON

Slow, and take third gear about 200 metres from line

Select left hand lane unless arrows indicate another lane

If light is green, keep going in third, but slow to second if it has been green a long time

If light changes to amber, stop if far enough away to be safe

If light is red or amber, stop at line. Use clutch and handbrake

Select first gear, unless you'll have to wait a long time

On red and amber, get ready to go

On green, go if way is clear

Watch for pedestrians and bikes

PROCEDURE FOR TURNING LEFT

Mirror and signal left

Slow. Take third gear 200 metres from line and then second

Select left hand lane

If main or filter light is green, keep going but wait for pedestrians on exit road

If light changes to amber, stop at line if you can do so safely

If light is red, stop at line and use clutch and handbrake

On red and amber, get ready to go

On green, turn if way is clear

Watch for pedestrians and bikes

PROCEDURE FOR TURNING RIGHT

Mirror and signal right

Slow to third gear about 200 metres from line, then second

Select right-hand lane

If light is green, enter junction and wait for traffic and pedestrians if necessary

If light changes to amber, stop if you've room to do so safely

If light is red or amber, stop at line and use clutch and handbrake

Select first gear, unless you will have to wait long enough to make neutral worthwhile

On red and amber, get ready to go

On green, enter junction and wait for gap in oncoming traffic and pedestrians crossing exit

TRAFFIC CAMERAS

Cameras on traffic lights spot people jumping red. Those in big metal boxes see people breaking the speed limit, usually by a lot; some speedometers have a 15 per cent error, so the cameras can't be exact. If either type catches someone it will flash and may take their picture, although there are not always cameras in the boxes. Those caught usually receive a letter within 14 days, but it may take longer. Rubber tubes across the road and vehicle or hand-held radar also catch speeders. Smaller cameras watch traffic.

ROUNDABOUTS

Roundabouts are meant to ease traffic flow by allowing vehicles to merge or cross without stopping. Many roundabouts have been altered, with traffic lights, changed priorities shown by 'Give Way' lines, extra roundabouts added to the outside, lanes cut through the middle and various other things to try and make them work. I describe the normal procedures below, but you must always be ready for variations. Look for signs on the approach. These will tell you which lane you need, and give some idea of altered layouts. Watch for 'Give Way' lines, and even on the roundabout be prepared to stop.

The rule is: **Give Way to Vehicles Coming From Your Right**. This means you must wait for a gap in the traffic on the roundabout. Arrive at the line in second gear and keep going if you can. If you must stop, select first gear and hold the clutch down ready. Use the handbrake if you will have to wait long. For a left turn you normally approach in the left lane and stay in it through the roundabout, signalling left all the time. You may think you only need a gap in the outside lane, but cars on the inside lane, hoping to leave at the next exit, will start signalling left as they pass you and will move left. Watch for bikes and horses, which often keep to the outside; pedestrians crossing exit roads; and long vehicles that need more room to turn (forgetting this can be a crushing experience). When in the outside lane, let cars from the inside cross in front of you. Keep to the left of your exit road.

When going ahead, you generally approach in the left one of two lanes and keep to it throughout. Don't indicate until you pass the exit before the one you want. If the left-hand lane's blocked, or signs or markings dictate, use the right-hand lane throughout. Generally you still leave to the left of your exit road, but if there are two lanes in the exit direction, you may take the right-hand one from the roundabout's inside lane, if it is safe and more convenient. If you have to cross the left-hand lane from the right, look in your mirrors (especially the passenger side door mirror) and glance over your left shoulder to make sure there's a gap to cross through. If there's not enough space, slow or wait, or go right around again.

If you are turning into a road on the right or are going all the way round, approach in the right-hand lane, signalling right. Change to the left indicator as you pass the exit before the one you want. Move across the outside lane and into the exit road as for going ahead.

MINI ROUNDABOUTS

Should be treated like normal roundabouts

These are usually white pimples in the road. They indicate that you must give way to traffic from the right and should be treated like normal roundabouts, through there won't usually be room to indicate left as you pass the exit before the one you want. It is OK, though better avoided, to drive over the white of the spot. Be careful: a car from the other direction may turn right, across your path, when you expected it to go straight on. Watch for people doing U-turns. At multiple mini roundabouts, don't enter the first one until you can get through the second one too. Often there is only room for one car at a time on mini roundabouts.

PROCEDURE
FOR GOING STRAIGHT AHEAD

- Check mirrors but don't signal
- Approach in left lane, or lane to the right if left one's blocked
- Slow to second gear
- Look to the right for a gap
- Look for people indicating
- Look for bikes
- If there's a gap, keep going
- If you stop, select first gear
- Keep to your lane right through
- As you pass exit before the one you want, signal left
- If not in outside lane, look in mirrors and over left shoulder for gap before moving to left
- If necessary, slow down or wait
- Enter new road well to left
- Make sure indicator has cancelled

PROCEDURE
FOR TURNING LEFT

- Check in your mirrors
- Signal left and keep it going
- Approach in left-hand lane
- Slow down to second gear
- Look to the right for a gap
- Look for people indicating
- Look both ways for bikes
- If there's gap, keep going
- If you stop, select first gear
- Keep using left lane and signal
- Enter new road well to left
- Make sure indicator has cancelled

PROCEDURE
FOR TURNING RIGHT

- Check mirrors
- Signal right
- Move to right-hand lane
- Slow to second gear
- Look to the right for a gap
- If there's a gap, keep going
- If you stop, select first gear
- Use roundabout's inside lane
- As you pass exit before the one you want, change to left signal
- Look in mirrors and glance over left shoulder before crossing outside lane
- Check for bikes and pedestrians
- Enter new road well to left
- Make sure indicator has cancelled

PEDESTRIAN CROSSINGS

Always be ready to stop

Pedestrians may cross the road anywhere, sometimes without warning, so always be alert, especially where you see children at the side of the road. In an ideal world, they would all cross at designated crossings.

On the approach to a crossing you should always be ready to stop, especially if there are people on the pavement near it. They may jump out without thinking (especially children). Watch for people with white sticks (visually impaired) and white sticks with red stripes (deaf too). If you are required to stop, try to brake gently, as normal, although if someone leaps out in front of you, you must do an emergency stop. Generally, though, you will have loads of time to show following drivers your brake light with early light braking, and to come to a gentle halt. You should be well back from the 'Stop' or 'Give Way' line so the pedestrian can see past you. Always apply the handbrake when waiting at the crossing in case your foot slips off the clutch (if you're still in gear) or you're bumped from behind. Never signal to the pedestrian to cross, as they may

have seen a problem you haven't. Don't try to hurry them by revving your engine, swearing, screaming, biting the steering wheel, etc. When you are waiting in a queue of cars, leave crossings clear. Just because you're in a traffic jam doesn't mean the pedestrians have to be.

Never overtake the moving vehicle closest to a pedestrian crossing, and don't stop on the approach, except to let people cross, or in emergencies. (It blocks people's view.) Most crossings have zig-zag lines for 25 metres to show where this applies, but you shouldn't stop even if they don't.

The Highway Code says you should give a hand signal before you start slowing at a zebra crossing to show what you intend to do. Even on the test, only do this if you will not need to steer with both hands and have plenty of time. You must keep both hands on the wheel while you are actually stopping. If the weather permits, keep your window open on the test to allow easy signalling. In practice, few drivers use hand signals. Your intentions should be clear by the way you are driving.

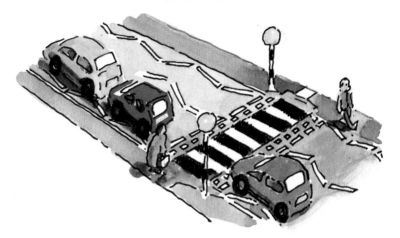

Zebra crossings

Zebra crossings have black and white stripes, continuously flashing beacons and zig-zag lines. They show where pedestrians have the right of way. An island in the middle of a zebra crossing makes it into two separate crossings, though stopping for someone who is still on the other side is polite, as is stopping for someone waiting at the kerb, especially if they have a pram, wheelbarrow, zebra etc. If someone puts a foot on the crossing, however, stopping is no longer a matter of good manners: you MUST stop for them. Use anticipation to make sure you don't need to squeal to an emergency stop.

Pelican crossings

These light-controlled pedestrian crossings get their name from PEdestrian LIght CONtrol. They use traffic lights to stop cars a short time after the button has been pressed. The difference from normal traffic lights is the flashing amber phase before green (instead of red and amber) meaning 'Give way to people on the crossing, but go if clear'. Pelican crossings have rows of studs to show where people should walk, and zig-zag lines to show the 'No Overtaking or Parking' zone. Even if there's an island in the middle, it's still one crossing unless the two halves are staggered. On puffin crossings, so-named because they are Pedestrian User (F)Friendly INtelligent, infra-red detectors hold the lights on red if anyone is on the crossing, or keep them green if there's no one in their range. Toucan crossings allow both pedestrians and bikes across, and also have no flashing amber. Normal traffic lights may have pedestrian signals too.

On approach, look for pedestrians' 'Wait' sign, showing the button's been pressed to stop the traffic.

School crossing patrols

Outside schools, a school crossing patrol may operate. The 'School Ahead' warning sign sometimes has amber lights, which flash when the patrol is in operation (so go slower). When there is a crossing patrol person ahead holding up their 'Stop' sign you must, of course, stop. You should also stop, however, when you see them standing at the side of the road with a group of children waiting to cross.

LEVEL CROSSINGS

Where the road crosses a railway line the rule is: always give way to trains. There are various kinds of level crossing, but some rules always apply. Never start on to the crossing unless your exit is clear, preferably with room for at least two cars so that someone breaking the next rule won't be caught out. There are often box junction markings to remind you of this. The next rule is: don't drive nose to tail over the crossing. Don't park on the approaches, and move away quickly after you've crossed, so you don't block an exit. As you cross, go fairly quickly. Glance both ways before you start. Never stop on the crossing.

When the amber light and audible alarm start, stop at the line if safe to do so, but keep going if you are already over it. Stop at the line when the red lights start flashing. If the red lights continue after the train has passed, then another train is on its way.

There's a phone for talking to the signalman. Call before crossing with anything big, slow (below 5 mph) or so low that it may scrape the crossing's hump. Also call before crossing with livestock. If you get permission to cross, ring again afterwards to say you made it. Also telephone if you break down on the crossing, if the lights keep going for more than five minutes without a train appearing, or at crossings with no lights, barriers or other indication of what's coming if you feel you cannot cross safely.

Between the warning sign and a concealed crossing, there will be three red countdown markers on the approach.

Never zig-zag round the barriers

PROCEDURE
IF YOU BREAK DOWN ON THE CROSSING

- Get all passengers out and off crossing
- Telephone the signalman
- Try to move car clear, if lights and alarms haven't started
- Phone again if you get clear
- If lights start, stand clear of crossing

DIFFERENT TYPES OF CROSSING

AUTOMATIC HALF BARRIER

These have amber then flashing red lights and an alarm. There is a telephone and barriers operated by the train block your side of the road.

The barriers drop just after the red lights start flashing. Never zig-zag around them.

AUTOMATIC OPEN

These have the amber and red lights and alarm, but no barriers. There will be the white diagonal cross sign, outlined in red.

Again, the lights work auto-matically as the train approaches, but there are no barriers to enforce the message, so be extra careful. You can cross when the lights go out (there's no green light) but look both ways first.

WITH GATES OPERATED BY ATTENDANT

These have barriers right across the road, usually with the red and amber lights and alarm.

The attendant will open the gates or barriers, possibly by remote control. Obey the lights as before. If there are no lights, don't enter the crossing after the barriers start to descend.

WITH GATES AND RED AND GREEN LIGHTS

You open the gates yourself. Tiny red and green lights operated by approaching trains tell you when.

Stop at the gate. Switch off and get out. If the light's red, wait for train. If green, open BOTH sets of gates fully; check light is still green; drive across; close gates. Remember to look both ways before walking or driving across, and use your ears.

WITH GATES BUT NO LIGHTS OR ATTENDANT

You must open the gates yourself. There's usually a railway telephone to call and check first.

Stop and get out, so you can hear better. Look for trains. Phone signalman to ask if one's coming. Open all gates fully. Check again for trains. Drive across. Close the gates. Phone signalman to say you're across.

OPEN

Nothing but red cross, 'Give Way' and 'Open Crossing' signs. No lights or gates.

Stop to look and listen for trains. If you can, get out to hear better. Then listen again with your engine idling just before crossing. Take extra care.

TRAMS

The trains have escaped and got on to the roads. What's more, often they are almost silent. Don't enter their lanes. When a tram is at a stop, watch for pedestrians (especially children) emerging from behind it. Watch for signs warning of where the tram lane crosses from one side of the road to the other. Treat this like a railway crossing, but remain in the car.

REVERSING TO THE LEFT

This shows you have the skill required to control the car in reverse. A real test would be to back between other cars (they may make you do that too) but then you might hit one!

Go very slowly, using the clutch at just above biting point to control speed. Removing the seat-belt is legal but normally unnecessary and may affect your insurance. Hold the steering wheel as normal. While you are moving in a straight line you can remove your left hand from the wheel and rest your arm on the back of the seats if this feels better, but you must have both hands on the wheel when you're turning. You must turn to look over your left shoulder, rather than steering in the mirror. (Shift in the seat at the start to get comfortable.) But also keep looking all around and be ready to stop. Everyone in the universe has priority over you because you are reversing against the traffic flow. Check over your right shoulder before the turn because the front of your car will swing out. Keep special watch for pedestrians, especially children, just behind the car who may be hidden from your view. Sometimes the only way is for you or a passenger to get out and look. It is usually unnecessary to signal: if there are other vehicles or pedestrians nearby you shouldn't continue to reverse, but give way. You should start and end around

50 cm from the kerb, though opinions vary. To learn to judge this: park at the correct distance (get out and check) on a straight road. Then turn in the seat as you would on the test, and see where the kerb crosses the bottom edge of the rear window. It will move away from here as you turn, but should return by the finish. Go backwards and then start to turn as the curving kerb moves to the edge of the rear window, or into the side window if the corner is sharp. Once round the bend, after straightening the wheels you will need to turn the other way slightly so that you are again going in a straight line, 50 cm or so from the kerb. If another car comes along, stop, or even move forwards to get out of its way.

It's an offence to reverse further than necessary. On the test, this is until the examiner tells you to stop (normally three or four car lengths). Stopping to correct yourself part-way through, or even pulling forwards a bit (after a proper look around) before carrying on, is not a serious fault; hitting or mounting the kerb is. Downhill you may need brake and clutch to control speed, instead of accelerator and clutch. Uphill, use reverse hill starts. Otherwise, the procedure on hills is the same. Practising a lot, on corners of varying sharpness, and later on slopes, will make this difficult procedure almost automatic.

BEAR IN MIND

- Keep looking around
- Only move back while looking back
- Watch for children behind car
- Go slow!
- Don't hit kerb
- If anyone comes along, stop
- No need to signal

PROCEDURE

- Glance down road as you pass it
- Stop 50 cm from kerb [1]
- Handbrake on and gear to neutral
- Look all round
- If clear, gear to reverse
- Look over left shoulder
- Clutch to biting point
- Handbrake off
- Look all round
- Move back until you reach corner
- Ease to stop, glance forward and to the right [2]
- Looking back over left shoulder, start moving again
- Left lock at corner [3]
- Turn corner
- Straighten up [4]
- Keep kerb at 50 cm point in window
- Reverse three car lengths [5]
- Stop [6]
- Handbrake and neutral gear

Reversing to the left

Look for pedestrians, especially children

REVERSING TO THE RIGHT

This is easier than reversing to the left, and much less common on the test. But if you have restricted vision to rear or sides, as in a van, this is probably what you'll have to do.

You'll be asked to stop before an opening to the right, and will be told what to do. Then after the normal starting procedure, mirror and signal a move to the centre of the road, opposite the side-road. Don't sit there signalling: people may think you're turning. Take the opportunity to look down the side-road. When there's no oncoming traffic, move to the other side of the major road. Stop with your driver's side 50 cm from the kerb, about 15 metres from the corner.

Have your window open so that when you turn to look over your right shoulder you can see the kerb. Adjust your position for comfortable reversing. Look over your shoulder, rather than steering in the mirror. Again: go very slowly, using the clutch to control speed. Keep looking all around and be ready to stop. Everything has priority over you. Check forward and over your left shoulder, and mirror before the turn because the front of your car will swing into the path of anyone unfortunate enough to be coming along. Stop if anyone's coming. Keep watch for pedestrians, especially children just behind the car who may have slipped in there while you weren't looking (remember, your

Everything has priority over you

vision behind is restricted). No signal is necessary.

Go backwards and then start to turn when you see that your back wheels have reached the corner. As with the reverse left, the exact place varies with the sharpness of the bend. Once around the bend, continue turning to move back in towards the kerb, before turning the other way slightly so that you come back again to a straight line, 50 cm out. If another vehicle appears, stop or move forwards for it.

Reverse until the examiner tells you to stop, or for the distance he told you to go back. You must be far enough from the junction to pull back to the left-hand side of the road, before turning normally at the corner. Put your seat-belt back on if you had removed it (remember you can do this although it could affect insurance), and don't forget to do your starting, and left- or right-turn procedures properly. As before, stopping and pulling forwards to correct yourself is much better than hitting the kerb. Downhill you may need the foot-brake to control speed, instead of the accelerator. Uphill you will be doing handbrake hill starts. Again: practise. If you don't feel confident while practising, you will feel worse on the test. However, unless you are going to be taking the test in a van, more practice should be done with the reverse on the left.

50 cm from the kerb

PROCEDURE

- Mirror and signal right [1]
- Move to centre of main road [2]
- Glance down side-road when opposite it
- When safe, move across road
- Stop 50 cm from kerb [3]
- Handbrake and neutral
- Open window and get comfortable
- Look all round
- If clear, gear to reverse
- Look over right shoulder
- Clutch to biting point
- Handbrake off
- Look all round
- Move back until rear is at corner
- Ease to stop, glance forward and over your left shoulder [4]
- Looking back over right shoulder, start moving again
- Right lock at corner
- Turn corner
- Straighten up [5]
- Keep at 50 cm from kerb
- Reverse four car lengths, stop [6]
- Apply handbrake and neutral gear

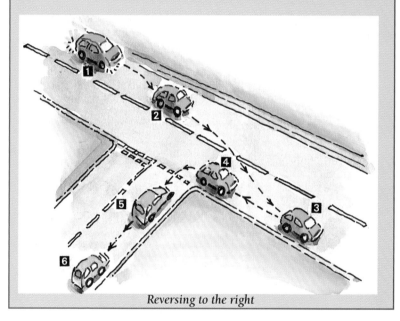

Reversing to the right

BEAR IN MIND

- *Keep looking around*
- *Only move back while looking back*
- *Watch for children behind car*
- *Go slow!*
- *Don't hit kerb (better to stop)*
- *If anyone comes along: stop*
- *No need to signal, but can before starting to turn right*

TURN IN THE ROAD

On the test this manoeuvre shows if you can control the car, but it's useful in real life too. When you're going the wrong way and want to turn around, it's best to take a quiet side-road and turn by backing into an opening. But if the side-road has no openings, you can turn in it using forward and reverse gears. This is often called a three-point turn, but on a narrow road you may need more than three.

The secret is to move slowly using clutch control, and steer briskly. Never turn the wheel while stationary. Move with the clutch at just above biting point. Since the road has camber you may need hill starts at the kerbs: use foot-brake and clutch to control speed, and handbrake until the clutch bites when starting. The tyres must not bump the kerb nor should the car overhang it. Don't indicate: there's no one to indicate to.

You'll be told to stop. Pick a spot with no obstructions on the road or pavements, such as trees, pillar boxes, driveways etc. Keep looking for cars and stop for them; only keep going to get out of their way.

Do the moving-off procedure, taking a look over your right shoulder. Then check also that there are no pedestrians on the path or crossing the road. First gear and find the clutch biting point. If clear, move slowly while turning the wheel hard right. You should have full right lock within a metre or so from the kerb. As you get almost to the other side, turn the wheel hard left in the last metre before you stop with the foot-brake and put the handbrake on. Go into reverse and, with clutch biting, look both ways and behind you. Start back slowly, looking over your left shoulder, with full left lock within the first metre. As you near the other kerb, look over your right shoulder. Turn the wheel hard right in the last metre. Stop and put the handbrake on. Select first gear and look both ways and check your mirrors. Steer right while moving slowly to straighten up on the other side of the road, facing the direction you came from.

U-TURNS

Turning around in one movement is rare and not expected by others, because wide enough roads are usually too busy. Don't do a U-turn in a one-way street, on a motorway, or if there's a 'No U-turn' sign. Ask: is the turn safe, convenient and legal? Use the MSM routine.

PROCEDURE

- Mirror
- First gear and clutch biting
- Glance over right shoulder
- Move slowly, getting right lock [1]
- Continue observations up and down the road
- Steer left one metre from other kerb [2]
- Stop, handbrake on
- Reverse gear and clutch to biting point
- Look left, right and behind
- Look over left shoulder
- Creep back, getting left lock
- As you near other kerb, look over right shoulder [3]
- Steer right one metre from kerb [4]
- Stop, handbrake on
- Look left and right
- Forwards while turning right [5]
- Reverse again if necessary

Look left and right

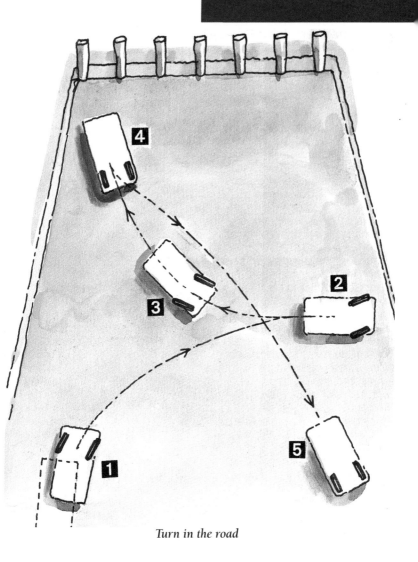

Turn in the road

- This is a useful manoeuvre to learn thoroughly
- Use quiet side-road for turning
- Pick a place without obstructions
- Nearby pedestrians may worry
- Stop to let other vehicles pass
- Don't turn wheel while stationary
- Move slow and turn wheel fast
- Slow with clutch and foot-brake
- Camber may mean hill starts
- Don't overhang or bump kerb

47

REVERSE PARKING

In a world with too many cars, you will often not have the luxury of a big space to park in, so you need to learn the extra manoeuvrability of reverse parking. This is included in the test, where it may replace one of the other reversing manoeuvres. You will usually be asked to reverse park behind a car in front, with no car behind. This may prevent some embarrassing bumps, but it means you will need more practice because the manoeuvre is difficult without anything to line up on. You will be expected to park within two car lengths, though with practice you'll only need one and a half.

You will be thinking about where you're going, but don't forget other road users. You could be an obstacle so before you start, look in your mirror and forwards (the front of your car may swing out) and signal left if necessary. Make sure it is safe before you start.

Stop parallel to, and a metre from, the parked car at the front of the space, and half a car length further forwards. The best position varies according to

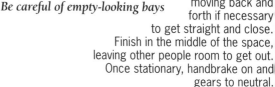

Be careful of empty-looking bays

the length of your car and the gap. Handbrake on and press the foot-brake to show your brake lights. Select reverse (another signal to other cars). Check all round. Adjust the position of your hands etc. for reversing and, looking over your left shoulder, bring the clutch to biting point. If it's still safe, release the handbrake and bring the clutch up a little more to start moving. Go very slowly throughout. Use slight left lock, and maybe more when the back of the car is in the space, watching the corner of the front parked car. If there is a car parked behind, try to line up the right side of your car with its left headlight. Remove the left lock, making sure you are clear of the car in front, then steer hard right to get parallel with the kerb and close to it, but don't touch or mount the kerb. Watch for pedestrians who may step out, thinking you've seen them. Straighten up the wheels, moving back and forth if necessary to get straight and close. Finish in the middle of the space, leaving other people room to get out. Once stationary, handbrake on and gears to neutral.

Parking in a car park

There's often little room to move in car parks so it's usually best to reverse into the space. This also lets you drive straight out when you go. Park between the lines, preferably near the middle of the space so the people on either side can open their doors. Read the signs on entry to find the system of payment, so you don't hold up traffic while trying to escape with the wrong change or a ticket that hasn't been through the special machine.

When looking for a space, be careful of empty-looking bays that have a motorbike or Mini in them. Also be careful when you are at the front of a queue of cars that are all looking for spaces; when you pull beyond the space ready to reverse, the car behind may nip in forwards behind you. In an indoor car park, use dipped headlights (but remember to turn them off after you park).

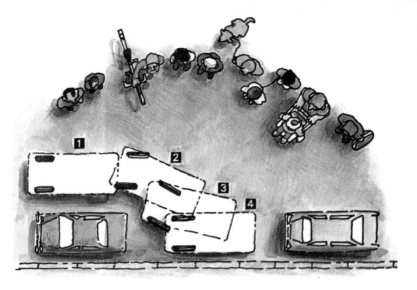

Watch for pedestrians

PROCEDURE

- Look forward and in mirror
- Signal left if necessary
- Stop one metre out from front car [1]
- Handbrake on, and foot-brake down
- Gear to reverse
- Check all round
- Position hands etc. for reversing
- Look over left shoulder
- Clutch to biting point
- If safe, brakes off and clutch up a little to start backwards
- Slight left lock [2]
- Watch corner of front car
- When clear, right lock [3]
- Move back and forth to adjust
- End in middle of space, near kerb [4]
- Handbrake on and select neutral

Park so the people on either side can open their doors

BEAR IN MIND

- You need at least one and a half car lengths
- Watch for other road users
- Watch for pedestrians
- Go very slowly

BEAR IN MIND

- *Always give way to traffic on the motorway*
- *Don't overtake on the slip road*
- *Get used to speeds on motorway before trying to overtake*
- *Avoid stopping*

NOT ALLOWED ON MOTORWAYS

Some vehicles are not allowed on motorways because they hold up traffic: learners (except HGV learners), pedestrians, cyclists, low-powered motorbikes, animals, light invalid carriages, agricultural vehicles, or slow vehicles carrying heavy loads (except with permission).

A1(M)

NO L·drivers (except HGV)
Motorcycles under 50cc
Mopeds.Pedal cycles
Invalid·carriages
Pedestrians.Animals

JOINING A MOTORWAY

You are not allowed to drive on a motorway until you have passed your test. But you will be expected to know about motorway driving.

You may join the motorway where it starts at a roundabout, or another road may become a motorway, but normally you'll join via a slip road. This may just become a new lane on the carriageway (especially when joining from another motorway), but normally it leads into an acceleration lane where you adjust your speed to the traffic before merging into it.

A red light on the slip road means you must not enter the motorway, so watch for these. As you approach the carriageway, look ahead and to the side to get an idea of the traffic. Mirror, and indicate right. I know you can only move right anyway but the flashing light will warn motorway traffic of your presence. Glance over your right shoulder for a gap, and adjust your speed to meet it. Speed up along the acceleration lane so you can enter the gap smoothly.

Cancel your indicator (the shallow angle means it probably won't cancel automatically) and make final adjustments to your speed. Get used to the motorway speeds before you attempt to overtake. You should avoid stopping at the end of the acceleration lane if you can, but if there is no gap in the traffic you may have to do so. Always give way to traffic on the motorway.

This is straightforward in principle, but it is a good idea to practise in good weather and light traffic conditions. Then you will be able to cope confidently with difficult conditions: rush-hour traffic, poor visibility, rain or darkness. Remember you can stop at the end of the acceleration lane if you need to, and if you miss the end you'll be on the hard shoulder, which is illegal and clumsy but it won't kill you. Even, or especially, in the rain, it's worth opening your window before you get to the acceleration lane, so you can see better.

Fitness for the motorway

Don't use a motorway if you're tired or ill. You mustn't use the hard shoulder to rest on, but must wait for a service area or an exit, and these may be a long way away. Make sure the car is well ventilated.

The car must also be fit. Check lights, instruments, brakes and steering. Make sure the tyres have the right pressures (look in the handbook), and are in good condition. Loads must be secure. Make sure the windscreen washers have plenty of water. Petrol, oil and water are all used more quickly at high speeds, so

Make sure the car is well ventilated

check them. Mirrors, including the one on the passenger's door, must be clean and properly adjusted.

PROCEDURE

- Look for red light on slip road
- Wind down window
- Look at the motorway traffic [1]
- Mirror, and signal right
- Look over right should for gap in traffic [2]
- Adjust speed to enter gap
- Merge into motorway traffic [3]
- Cancel signal and adjust speed [4]
- If no gap, wait at end of lane

DRIVING ON MOTORWAYS

Getting where you're going is quick and easy on a motorway, but high speed means accidents happen quickly, too. Be especially cautious.

Anticipate: you can avoid being involved in a crash if you keep watching well ahead and in your mirrors. If you see things like bunched vehicles or flashing lights, slow gently but never brake hard. A brief flash of your hazard warning lights will warn following drivers of the hazard. See and obey all the signs and signals. Some places still just have flashing amber lights. These mean 30 mph. Don't drive too near someone's tail as this gives you no chance to stop. Even in good conditions leave a two-second gap. Make that four when wet and twenty when icy. Always use headlights at night or in bad visibility. Only use rear fog-lamps if visibility is below 100 metres.

Be polite; avoid conflict. Help

Keep looking in your mirror

drivers joining from slip roads by changing lane or adjusting speed. Try to help people who are changing lane. Make life easier for others, as you hope they'll do for you.

Emergencies and breakdowns

If you break down or you're suddenly unfit to drive, stop on the hard shoulder. With bad steering, hold the wheel tightly. If the brakes fail, slow gently to the shoulder. Stop on the left, away from traffic. Try to stop near a phone. Use hazard warning lights, and sidelights at night.

Get the passengers out on to the verge by nearside doors only. Get adults out first to control any children. Leave the dog inside. Put a red triangle 150 metres behind the car. The phones

Leave the dog inside

are a mile apart and posts every 100 metres point to the nearest one. Leave the passenger door unlocked. Keep as far from the traffic as you can (don't cross roads), and remain alert for danger while calling. The phone connects to the police. Mention your breakdown organisation if you are in one. (You should be!) Say if you're alone, especially if you're a woman. Disabled drivers should display a 'Help' pennant, and only go to a phone if one is very near.

Wait on the verge by the car with the door unlocked. Get in and lock the doors if someone comes. Talk through a small gap at the top of a window. Say you've called the police. People sent to help will know about you and have identification. Being hurt by a car is five times as likely as being attacked. When you rejoin traffic, speed up on the shoulder.

Officially you should not try any repairs yourself, and if something falls from the car you must call the police rather than retrieving it.

ROADWORKS AND CONTRAFLOWS

'Contraflow' literally means against the flow. To be precise, this is when traffic going one way is directed along a lane of the other carriageway closed to its normal traffic. What matters is that when roadworks are needed, the rest of the motorway is divided fairly to keep traffic flowing.

For instance the dreaded cones block two of a carriageway's three lanes, so the remaining lane, plus three in the other direction and two hard shoulders, are shared out. Signs show the temporary layout and speed limits. There may be special yellow catseyes to guide traffic in lanes.

Don't drive a long way looking sideways

Lanes and overtaking

Many normal driving skills aren't needed on the motorway. They're replaced by one important skill: lane discipline. You will, however, need to remain alert and maintain your concentration, perhaps longer than usual, without the benefits of continually changing circumstances to keep you awake. To turn off, you use the left-hand and deceleration lanes. To change motorways you select the appropriate lane at the interchange and it carries you automatically on to the other road. To overtake, you take a lane on the right until you're past the slower-moving vehicle.

1. Always use all your mirrors, and signal your intention to switch lanes. Do this early, and repeat it for each lane change if you want more than one. A second look in the mirror helps you judge the speed of following cars.

2. Glance quickly over your shoulder into your blind spot before you change lane, but don't drive a long way while looking sideways.

3. Look for cars coming up fast in the lane you want to enter, especially if it's on your right, or cars moving over at the same time as you. If going faster than the car in front of them, they may intend to overtake. Watch for cars moving back to the middle lane from the right-hand lane.

4. You'll probably have to cancel the signal manually, as the automatic cancel won't work on shallow angles.

5. Don't cut in. Don't move over until you can see the following car in your interior mirror. Someone on the left may flash their headlights to invite you into the gap in front of them, but they may just be warning you, or a driver they intend to overtake, that they're there. Be careful; make your own decisions.

6. All lanes but the left-hand one are for overtaking. You can stay in a middle lane when passing a string of slower vehicles, but move back when the left is clear. If there are more than two lanes, some traffic such as lorries or cars towing caravans, mustn't use the right-hand one. If, you block the middle lane they will not be able to overtake, so be considerate.

7. Don't overtake on the left.

8. Hills may have crawler lanes for slow-climbing, heavy vehicles. Try not to block their return to the normal left-hand lane.

9. Keep to the centre of your lane. Only change lanes if you must. Take it gently so you and others have time to see what's happening.

LEAVING A MOTORWAY

Unless you want to go where the motorway ends, you'll usually leave it via a slip road on the left. This will have a deceleration lane so you can get off the main carriageway without slowing the traffic. You enter this from the left-hand lane. If you are in an overtaking lane, move over early, going one lane at a time. Use the Mirror Signal Manoeuvre routine for each lane change. Don't cross the hard shoulder. Once in the deceleration lane start slowing, but don't change gear until you're well into the slip road. You should keep checking your speedometer as you'll feel you're going slower than you really are (maybe by 20 mph), and there are sharp turns ahead. Check your speed before changing gear.

A mile before the exit there'll be a sign telling you which road it leads to, and what the junction number is. You should know all the junction numbers for your journey; then you can just look for your number. After this first sign, move into the left-hand lane by the next sign, at half a mile, which is like the last one but with the destination of the exit named. There are countdown markers at 300 yards (270 metres) from the start of the deceleration lane, then at 200 and 100 yards. Mirror and start to signal left between 300 and 200 yards. At the start of the deceleration lane there's another sign telling you what the others said plus your destination if you stay on the motorway. The pattern of signs may be different where exits are close together.

After you leave the motorway you will see an 'End of Motorway' sign where the rules change back to normal roads so you may have to face cyclists, two-way traffic, roundabouts and all that.

You may also leave when the left lane goes to another destination, but this usually only takes you on to another motorway. This will be well signposted. It's important to take the correct lane, as the turn-off lane will go straight into the other motorway.

BEAR IN MIND

- If you miss your exit, you'll just have to go to the next one
- Move over one lane at a time
- Don't cross the hard shoulder
- Get most of your slowing down done in the deceleration lane
- After leaving, you'll feel you're going slower than you are
- Leave gear change till you have checked your speedometer
- Know your junction numbers

PROCEDURE

- Move to the left-hand lane at the first direction sign (MSM as you change lanes)
- Be in the left lane by second sign [1]
- Mirror, and signal left after first countdown marker [2]
- Move into deceleration lane [3]
- Cancel indicator
- Slow down [4]
- Check speedometer
- Slow down some more

You and your car need a rest

SERVICE AREAS

These are the only places you can park on the motorway. Follow the usual procedure for leaving a motorway and the normal joining procedure afterwards. Remember to slow down, and that other people may not slow enough, so be careful in the car park. As ever, take or hide valuables, and lock the car.

Service areas have food, fuel, toilets and so on. You and the car need a rest every couple of hours, if possible, and usually this means not missing a single set of services.

55

NIGHT DRIVING

It's exciting, driving through the night, headlights probing the darkness ahead. Many film dramas have started like this, normally just before the car dramatically crashes. The main problem of driving in the dark is that you can't see as much or as far ahead as in daylight. (Well, who'd have thought it?) Those high beam headlights only reach about 100 metres ahead, and dipped headlights don't do half that. Unless the road is very well lit, this is the distance in which you must be able to stop.

Of course, there are some advantages which you can use. You may be able to see vehicles coming from over hills and around corners because their headlights will be visible. However, you should never rely on this if you need to overtake; other drivers may not have their headlights on. Roads will often be clearer after dark, but don't be tempted to go faster.

There are disadvantages, of course. There may be pedestrians in the shadows, or hazards in the unlit road. Someone may think they are visible because they are wearing fluorescent clothes, when in fact these only help at twilight and are useless at night. A cyclist may be

Headlights probing the darkness

riding along without lights, or even with lights that are difficult to see. Because your eyes are adapted to the pool of light from your headlights, you will be unable to see into those dangerous shadows. The only answer is to drive slower, and be especially careful.

CORNERS

Always use dipped lights at a junction. If you want to warn other people that you're about to appear around the bend, flash your lights. You must

not use your horn at night in built-up areas, unless stationary and in danger from a moving vehicle. (And no banging doors or revving engines: don't you know people are trying to sleep?) Flash your lights instead. Waiting at the corner, don't sit there with your foot on the brake, because your brake light will dazzle people behind you. Use the handbrake instead (but don't use it for stopping). Remember that when you look sideways to see if anyone is coming, your eyes will still be adjusted to the bright lights in front rather than the unlit shadow. You may not see a car which only has sidelights on, especially if you are distracted by a more sensible person behind who is using dipped headlights. Watch very carefully for pedestrians and cyclists.

SEEING AND BEING SEEN

SEE Being dazzled is less likely with a clean windscreen. You'll also see better if you don't have tinted windows or dark glasses. Get regular eye checks. When you leave a brightly lit place, such as a motorway service area, give your eyes a few minutes to adjust before driving.

BE SEEN Clean the lights and reflectors and check that they are in good working order. Keep spare bulbs in the car.

BEAR IN MIND

- *Use the correct lights*
- *Drive more slowly*
- *Do not rely on others' lights before manoeuvring*
- *Watch out for pedestrians and cyclists*
- *Slow down or stop if dazzled*

The lights to use

In general, when things start getting a bit dim, switch on dipped headlights. From lighting-up time you must have them on except in very well-lit town roads, where sidelights are legal. But even here, dipped headlights are better. You should light up before you have to in twilight, and switch off in the morning after the time the law says you may. The amount of extra time you have your lights on for should increase if your car is a dark colour.

When should you use high beam? Any time you won't dazzle others and you're not in town (where roads are slower and well lit). When high beam is on, a blue light on the dashboard comes on. If someone comes in the opposite direction you should dip your lights so you don't dazzle them. This has the added advantage that other drivers see you dip your lights, and may be reminded to dip theirs. If not and you are dazzled, concentrate on the road lit by your lights rather than staring at theirs. If you still can't see properly, slow down or even stop. Don't deliberately dazzle other drivers to get your own back. Remember that a heavy load at the back of your car, or driving uphill, may tip the front up, so the lights dazzle others. Check the road and verge ahead before dipping in case a hazard is coming up.

When you're behind someone, use dipped beam and don't drive too close. When the driver behind doesn't dip, the reflection in your mirror may dazzle you. Move the mirror or use the anti-dazzle lever on it, which cuts down the amount of light it reflects. Once the glare has gone, put the lever back to normal, because on anti-dazzle the mirror doesn't allow you to see much more than people's lights. When you are at the front of the queue, use high beam. Then if someone wants to pass they can see what's coming. As they pass, dip your lights. They should have been using dipped lights as they passed. Remember that even dipped lights may dazzle if you get too close.

Your rear fog-lamps should only be used when visibility is below 100 metres. Otherwise they will dazzle people behind you, and make your brake lights less obvious. Don't keep your foot on the brake when stationary or you will dazzle people behind you.

A heavy load at the back may tip front up

57

POOR VISIBILITY

The most dangerous thing to encounter on the road is reduced visibility: this means heavy rain, fog, snow, or smoke. Try to avoid driving in these conditions, but if you can't, allow more time for the journey. The main things to remember are to see and be seen, and to pick a speed where you can stop within the distance you can see. Be prepared for other drivers who – unlike you – drive too close, go too fast and don't wait for proper gaps, whatever the conditions. The worse the visibility, the more dangerous they become.

Some people think they must do 70 mph on the motorway if signs don't display a lower limit. This is not

The road markings may be less clear

Allow more time for the journey

true. Pick your own speed so you can see your stopping distance. In thick fog this may be very slow. Mirror before slowing, and then use light braking to display brake-lights. Remember that speeds and distances will be harder to judge. Don't hang on to the lights of the car in front, because it may brake for something you can't see, and you may not be able to stop quickly enough to avoid hitting it. In very bad visibility (below 100 metres) you should use rear fog-lights, but this makes brake-lights, including those of the car in front, harder to see. The road markings may be less clear, but they are what you must use to find your way.

In bad visibility, used dipped headlights. Don't use high beam, as

this dazzles the person in front, and also reflects back from the fog into your eyes. Legally you may use sidelights with fog-lights, but it's still better to have head-lights on as well. This is as much to be seen as to see. Keep the windows and lights clear. Use demisters and windscreen wipers.

When waiting to turn right, signal early. Open your window and turn the radio off so you can listen. Using the horn appropriately may help others know you're there. Keep you foot on the brake to keep your brake-lights on.

Be careful in patchy fog. It may look like no more than light mist until you hit a fog bank and everything goes white. This is especially common on motorways and country roads. River crossings are where the fog often likes to hang around. Don't speed up between thick patches.

Be careful in patchy fog

SEE AND BE SEEN

It's bad enough having fog outside, without having another layer inside the window. When it's cold or damp the windows mist up quickly and you need your demisters. These are mainly for the windscreen, but may blow on side windows too. An electric rear window heater is also useful. Electrically-heated front windscreens are rare but useful, especially when freezing fog is clinging to everyone else's glass. An open window will help prevent misting, but remember you can't steer well with frost-bite. Rain, fog and spray from other vehicles

An open window will help

cover the glass in a layer of water which distorts vision, but before you use the wipers, consider whether the glass is wet enough for them to slide without smearing or scratching. If not, use the washer first. In cold weather the wipers may freeze to the glass.

Before the journey, wipe the lights and windows (not with the same cloth: road dirt may scratch the windows). Ask passengers to clear bits that the car's demisters aren't getting to while going along, but don't let them distract you.

Ice needs scraping off before you start. If it may be icy the next day, cover the windows the night before to avoid this. A layer of ice on the windscreen, even a thin one that you didn't notice you'd left after the scraping, can become a solid wall of light that you cannot see anything through when sunlight shines on it.

Never go with a light (rear, head or fog) not working. Other drivers may think the remaining one is attached to a motorbike.

REMEMBER
IN POOR VISIBILITY

- Dipped headlights
- Visibility under 100 metres: fog-lights
- Wipers and demisters
- Mirror and slow
- Slow using gentle brake
- See your stopping distance
- Don't hang on to car in front
- Speeds and distances are deceptive
- Waiting to turn: brake-lights and open window
- Careful of patchy fog
- Don't drive unless you must

Special poor visibility conditions

Generally you treat all bad visibility the same, but sometimes there are special points to bear in mind. In rain, snow or even some fog, the roads will be slippery, so stopping distances will increase. Freezing fog sticks to the outside of your windows like glue, and the only answer may be to stop and clean it off. Snow may be too heavy for the wipers, so again you will have to clean it off by hand.

Warm weather and bright sunlight may seem like good conditions, but having the sun in your eyes can stop you seeing properly, especially when the sun is low in the sky. Keep your windows clear with wipers and washers, and this includes clearing away summer's insects. Glare is worse with a dirty window. Use your car's

BEAR IN MIND

- Avoid skids by driving gently
- Use high gears, except downhill
- Finish braking before manoeuvre
- Only use clutch when you must
- Take corners slowly
- Steady speed going uphill
- Beware of others going too fast
- Undisturbed snow has more grip
- Black ice is invisible and glassy
- Beware of:
    wet roads, mud or leaves
    ice or snow
    loose chippings
    oil or grease
- Especially bad are:
    black ice
    melting snow/ice
    rain after dry spell

Each tyre touches the road across a footprint-sized area. Like a foot, the bit on the road shouldn't slide, and if it does you're in trouble.

When you ask the tyres to do something like slow down, speed up, turn, pull you uphill or slow you going down, they must push against the road. If they lose their grip and skid they may stop moving in the direction they turn, and you'll lose control. This is more likely when the road's slippery due to rain, ice, leaves, mud, loose chippings, or anything else that reduces grip. Black ice, where rain freezes as it lands, is especially lethal because it's invisible. Rain makes the road very slippery when it's just started after a dry spell as it mixes with the dirt that washes away later. Melting ice or snow is also very bad. Worn or wrongly inflated tyres help cause skids.

On slippery roads, slow down and increase the gap between vehicles. Use twice the gap in the wet and ten times on ice. All braking should be light. Go even slower on bends. Finish braking before reaching a bend. Never brake and steer at the same time. Slow into the bend; come out of it using gentle acceleration. Careful where the camber tips you outwards.

Ease acceleration up and down gently, and in the highest gear possible, especially when starting. Do everything slowly and gently. Slow, and get a lower gear, before reaching a down hill. Arrive at an up hill in the highest gear that'll take you all the way up, and keep a steady speed. In snow, the stuff nobody else has driven on yet has more grip.

If you start to skid, don't brake! Ease off the accelerator. If the back of the car is moving sideways, steer the front wheels the same way, so they point in the direction the car's moving. In other words, turn the wheel left if the back moves left. In the worse front-wheel skid, or the four-wheel drift this may lead to, you still turn into the skid but harder: steer right if the front's moving right. Turn back when you regain control.

If you go too fast in the wet, you may start aquaplaning. Here the tyres aren't even touching the road, but are riding a hump of water. The steering will feel light. You'll have little or no control. Keep straight and don't brake. Ease off the accelerator until back on the road.

If a tyre blows out, hold the wheel very tight to keep control. Don't brake hard, but stop gently at the roadside.

PROCEDURES

Procedure if you skid

- Release the brake
- Ease off the accelerator
- Steer so the wheels point the way the car is moving

Turn your wheels in the direction of the skid

Procedure if you aquaplane

- Don't brake
- Keep going straight
- Ease off accelerator

Procedure if a tyre blows

- Grip wheel to keep control
- Don't brake hard
- Roll to halt at side of road

Floods and fords

At a ford, or where the road is liable to flood, there may be a depth gauge. Otherwise you must judge for yourself whether the water is too deep for the car. If you think it is shallow enough, go very slowly in first gear. Have the engine going fast and the clutch slipping. If you go fast you will cause a wave which will flood the engine and soak nearby pedestrians. Diesel engines can ltake a bit of water but petrol ones are less tolerant. Keep to the shallowest part, which will probably be the crown of the road. Remember that if you stall half-way across, the passers-by you've just sprayed with water will laugh and refuse to help, so you will have to paddle to get assistance. Once through, mirror, and then dry your brakes by going slowly while pressing the pedal lightly. Test the brakes before speeding up.

If you go fast you will cause a wave

FITNESS TO DRIVE

You should never drive if you feel tired, very upset or otherwise unwell. Of course, we are not always bright and sparky, especially when crawling into work on Monday morning, or struggling home through the rain with a load of shopping. In practice, most people know when they feel bad and drive more carefully to make allowance. Under those circumstances, only drive if you must. If you're tired, ill (even a head cold affects driving), angry or upset, you will be less observant and more unpredictable. Consider whether you are fit to drive, perhaps taking time to compose yourself before you start. Go slower, slow down earlier, allow more time and take things easy.

If you feel tired while driving, open a window for air. Keep moving your gaze so your brain stays alert. If you can, stop and walk around.

Remember that positive feelings can also affect your driving, and a conscious decision to take care is needed. If you feel elated, for example, you may want to go fast, but know you mustn't. Never drive under the influence of drink or drugs. They often make driving illegal, and even below the legal limit for alcohol you will not be up to sober standards. Ask your doctor or pharmacist about prescribed or over-the-counter medicines. Some medicine labels warn you about possible drowsiness. Obviously you must try them to see if they cause this before you try to drive.

A surprising source of distraction is smoking, not because it's bad for your health, but because cigarettes can also dump a load of hot ash in your lap. If you know anything more distracting than having your trousers set on fire, I do not wish to hear about it.

Alcohol

Alcohol is a depressant. Its affects include lower inhibitions, which is why people often think it's a stimulant. Even a small amount slows reactions and dulls senses and co-ordination. All this when even sober drivers cannot always react fast enough. Even after one lunch-time wine and well under the legal limit, your driving will still be worse than normal. If a crisis occurs, your slow reactions will be less able to cope. Unfortunately, another effect of drink is to relax you and make unimportant things like smooth gear changes seem easier. So some people think they drive better after a drink; they are dangerously wrong.

Here are some facts. Some of the alcohol in your drink enters the blood via the stomach, but most goes into the intestines first. Your liver cleans it from your blood at about one unit an hour. One glass of wine or measure of spirits, or half a pint of normal-strength beer contains about one unit. Spirits are absorbed more slowly because they have trouble leaving the stomach, but high alcohol content normally means quick absorption. Sparkling wine gets you drunk quicker than still.

"We are not always bright and sparky"

You also get drunk quicker on an empty stomach.

The legal limit is 80 mg/100 ml of blood. At the limit, you are twice as likely to crash as when sober. Don't just guess whether or not you are over the limit. It is best not to drink any alcohol at all if you are driving. Under no circumstances should you drive if you are in any doubt. And remember that even the morning after you have been drinking, your blood may still contain enough alcohol to put you over the limit.

The police may make you take a breath test if there's reason to think you're drunk and intend to drive, or if you're driving in a way that suggests you may be. If you refuse the test you'll lose your licence anyway.

Cars are hard, but some soft squishy things also use the road. They're called people and animals. This includes you and your passengers, so wear your seat belts. Small children have special restraints (see Highway Code). Making sure under-fourteens use belts is the driver's responsibility.

Less well-protected people, outside the car, may do silly things. It's down to you, the tough one, to keep them safe. When turning, imagine there are two extra lanes to cross: bikes passing near the kerb, and pedestrians crossing the road you're turning into. You must wait for a gap in this 'traffic' too. If a driver stops to let you turn right, he may not have noticed the bike passing him on his left, but you must. Go slowly and carefully. In residential roads, go slow enough to stop quickly (below 15 mph).

PEDESTRIANS

Pedestrians can be unpredictable, especially children. They may step into the road without looking. So when there are crowds on the pavement, slow down and try to keep further from the kerb. In the rain, be even more careful because they may dash out. Remember they can be almost invisible at night. A honk may warn pedestrians, but don't alarm them, especially when it's slippery. Be considerate: don't splash through puddles and soak people.

Be very careful of children, who are more interested in their games than in traffic, and whose judgement of speed and distance may not be properly developed. Be careful of your own judgement too: your brain may mistake a small child nearby for an adult further away. Drive slowly in residential roads where children often play, and take special care around school start and end times. Regard a running child as a warning sign; they can change direction quickly. Watch for anyone, but especially children, appearing from behind buses, parked cars, or ice-cream vans. Look under these for little legs, and go at a speed from which you could stop.

Anybody, but especially children, may forget what they've learned and step on to a crossing without looking. People often cross the road at junctions. If they're crossing the road you're entering, stop and give way to them.

The elderly may also have bad judgement of speed and distance, and they can't always get out of the way quickly. They may also have a problem with hearing or seeing. A white stick means its carrier is visually impaired, and if the stick has red bands they are also deaf.

ANIMALS

Treat any animal as a risk. Farm animals may be herded along roads, so take care on country lanes, and obey people in charge of animals. In town, cats and dogs are more common and may make a last-moment dash across the road. Some places have signs where wild animals may cross. Be careful: they've as much right there as you, but don't screech to a halt so fast you cause a crash.

Go slowly and quietly past any animal, but especially horses. If the rider's having trouble, stop while they sort it out. Groups of riders probably include some learners.

If you knock down an animal, report this to the police if it's a horse, farm animal or a dog. You don't have to report a wild animal, although you do have a moral responsibility to try to avoid them, and help if they're hurt.

In the car: keep animals under control. They should be suitably restrained.

Cyclists

Bikes get everywhere. You struggle to leave a wide gap as you pass them (as you must). Then they overtake on your left at the next set of lights. They may creep by on your left when you're turning left (or right when you're going right), and are especially hard to see head on, so watch for them if turning or emerging.

Remember many cyclists are children, and although a proficiency test exists, they may not have taken it, nor even have read the Highway Code. They may wobble when dodging a drain or if hit by a crosswind, or because they're trying to carry a load. Uphill they may wobble and weave through tiredness. They may even have to stop and walk. A look over their shoulder may mean they intend to turn or move out.

Much of this also applies to motorbikes, especially the bit about being hard to see.

Think once, think twice, think bike.

Knowing how a car works helps you to develop car sympathy, which helps you to drive better and pass the test. Also, a knowledge of car mechanics means you can save money doing some of the simpler maintenance yourself, or take action if you break down.

Cars have become more complex as they've become easier to use, but the basic principles remain the same.

The basic layout is this: fuel is mixed with air in the carburettor. This petrol/air mixture is sucked into each of several cylinders in turn, compressed by the cylinder's piston and then lit by a spark from the spark-plug. The resulting explosion pushes down the piston, which turns a crank, which joins to the gearbox through the clutch and on through various links to the wheels. The piston shoves out the fumes from the explosion via a system of valves to the exhaust pipe.

The turning engine also generates electricity to charge the battery and make the sparks. The sparks ignite at different times, and are controlled by a distributor which switches them on and off in turn.

The cooling sytem pumps water (or in some cars, air) around the engine, then through the radiator to cool down again. The radiator is cooled by a fan which the engine turns with the fan belt. Other things such as the alternator and water pump are also turned by the fan belt. A temperature gauge or high temperature warning light on the dashboard tells you when the cooling's not working well enough.

The lubrication system keeps everything running smoothly by pumping around oil from the sump. An oil pressure warning light tells you when this isn't working properly.

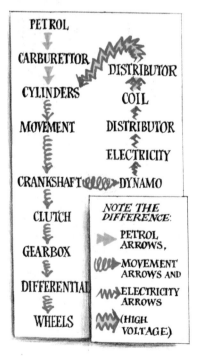

Flow chart of the engine system

Carburettor

The carburettor is a mixing machine, but it works more like an atomiser spray. Petrol from the tank is pumped into it and fills a small bottle called the 'float chamber'. The float keeps the right amount of petrol in the bottle by stopping it when there's enough but letting more in when needed. From here, suction from the cylinders pulls the fuel through a jet which sprays it, mixing it with air sucked in through the air filter. The result is an explosive petrol/air mixture which goes on to the cylinders.

The accelerator works a valve in the outlet from the carburettor, changing the amount of petrol/air mixture to go on to the next stage. The choke works a valve in the air inlet, making the mix richer in petrol by restricting the amount of air allowed in.

CYLINDERS

These are the engine's heart, where fuel becomes movement. Each cylinder holds a piston, and has at least two valves and a spark-plug at the top. They use a 'four-stroke' cycle.

Stroke 1: The valve to the carburettor opens and the piston is pulled down, sucking fuel (petrol/air) into the cylinder.

Stroke 2: The valve closes and the piston is pushed up, compressing the fuel. The spark-plug sparks (like a gas lighter), making the fuel explode.

Stroke 3: This causes a rapid expansion of gas which forces the piston down.

Stroke 4: The other valve (to the exhaust) opens and the rising piston pushes the fumes out. The valve closes ready for the next Stroke 1.

The pistons are joined to the crank shaft. As each of the four (or more) cylinders fires on stroke 3, they push the shaft round like a leg pushing a bicycle pedal. The spinning shaft turns the clutch plates to make the car go, and also pushes or pulls the other pistons on their strokes 1, 2 and 4. A flywheel on the shaft smooths the motion. The valves are on springs, and are pushed open by the turning camshaft (bar with bumps on it).

Electrical system

The engine turns a dynamo or alternator (like a motor in reverse) to make electricity. This 12-volt supply powers all the electrics, including the ignition. The battery stores electricity. It provides some for the starter motor and is charged during normal driving.

In the ignition sytem, the distributor's contact breaker points close and open to switch the 12 volts on and off. This makes an electrical pulse which is sent to the coil, where its voltage is increased. It returns to the distributor via thick high-tension leads. It is fed to the rotor arm which touches contacts for each cylinder in turn, sending a pulse along each lead that needs it. A push-on cap joins the lead to the spark-plug where the pulse flashes between contacts like lightning, lighting the fuel.

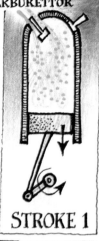

CARBURETTOR

STROKE 1

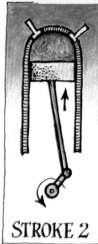

STROKE 2

BANG

STROKE 3

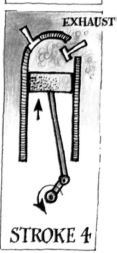

EXHAUST

STROKE 4

The four-stroke cycle

TURNING THE WHEEL

The crankshaft's motion goes on through the clutch, gearbox, differential and driveshafts, via universal joints to the front wheels.

Each gear allows a certain number of engine turns for every turn of the drive shaft. Top gear (usually fourth) turns them at the same speed. Overdrive turns the drive faster than the engine.

On bends, the outside wheel goes further than the inside. The differential allows for this by sending more of the motion to the outside wheel.

Don't do anything unless your sure of what you're doing

Unless it's new, you must put your car into the garage for MOT (Ministry of Transport) testing every year. However, it also needs a regular service to help prevent things from going wrong in between, and to keep everything working efficiently. You can save money doing some of this yourself, but there are also things that need checking more often than the annual service. Don't try anything unless you're sure of what you're doing, especially on a car with a modern engine management system, which requires a professional for most repairs. Buy a workshop manual for your model of car. Check the vehicle's guarantee to make sure you won't be violating it, and consult the handbook to see what needs regular attention. The following is a general guide if you aren't told anything different.

There are things that should be checked every week. (Most of this involves checking the levels of various fluids. Do this when the engine is cold.)

1. Check the tyre pressures (see box).
2. Check there's enough water in the radiator, or the expansion tank (bottle attached to the radiator) if there is one. In cold weather (in some modern cars, always) about a third of the coolant should be anti-freeze rather than water. If the water in the system freezes it expands and may crack the engine block.
3. Fill the windscreen washer bottle.
4. Check the oil in the sump. This lubricates the engine. The dip-stick should be pulled out, wiped, put in and taken out again. The level of the oil can be seen on it. If it is below the minimum level, put more oil in through the sump cap.
5. Check brake and clutch fluid (usually the same thing). They have two small bottles which you should top up. If either is losing a lot of fluid, have the system checked by a professional.
6. Check the lights, brakes, horn etc.

Also, if you have the service manual to tell you how, changing the circuit breaker points and the spark-plugs every 5000 miles is not difficult.

Check the lights, brakes, horn etc

TYRES

Check your tyres regularly with a pressure gauge and pump them up if they're soft. Check the tread. It must be at least 1.6 mm deep across the width of the tyre and all the way around. If wear is uneven, something may be wrong with the suspension or steering, so get professional help. Make sure there are no cuts or bulges in the tyre walls.

There are two main types of tyre: cross-ply and (more modern) radial-ply. Don't mix them. Cross-plies on the front and radials on the back is OK (just), but if you need to use the spare, you could then have different types on one axle, which is illegal.

Make sure there are no bulges

PETROL

Don't let the petrol tank get near empty before filling it because sediment will get into the fuel system.

Know where your petrol filler cap is so you can stop on the appropriate side of the pumps. Turn off the engine and don't smoke.

Unleaded fuel is thought better for the environment, but some cars need four star to work properly. It may be possible to convert to unleaded. (Ask your mechanic.) If you have a catalytic converter you must use unleaded; four star will ruin it. Never put diesel in a petrol car or vice versa.

Know where your filler cap is

SAFETY

Wait for everything to cool down before you work on the car. Oil and the water in the radiator, particularly, get scaldingly hot.

Be very careful about fire. There are lots of inflammable things on a car (especially the petrol). The battery may give off hydrogen, which is explosive. Don't smoke when you're working on the car.

There are many toxic things on a car. Don't let petrol, oil or other fluids stay on your skin for long. Be careful you aren't overcome by vapours, and never siphon liquids by sucking (you may swallow some). Carbon monoxide in exhaust fumes is lethal. The fumes sink in air, so be careful of

Don't let anything dangle

inspection pits under the car which could fill up with invisible gas. Brake-lining dust is also bad if breathed in.

Never go under a car it it's only held up by a jack. Be very careful when the car is running: the electricity in some high tension leads is enough to kill. Don't let anything dangle into moving machinery.

BREAKDOWNS

If your car is well maintained you'll have fewer breakdowns, but they are not all preventable. Joining a motoring organisation is a good precaution.

The first thing to do when you break down is consider other drivers. Get your car as far off the road as possible and let people know it's there. Get right off the road if you can. If you're moving when the engine dies, coast to the side of the road or on to the hard shoulder, and stop. (Brake gently, grip the wheel hard.) If it dies when stationary (e.g. at a junction) you may be lucky enough to get help to push it clear. If you push by yourself you must steer too, so hold the steering with one hand and push against the door frame with the other. If you must get out of the way immediately even if it means hurting the car (e.g. on a level crossing), you can use the starter motor. Go into gear and turn the starter to move the car electrically. This may damage the car, but not as much as having it hit by a train.

Use hazard lights to warn others. Tell people pushing not to hide the lights, and don't let anyone block them once you're at the roadside. Put a red warning triangle 50 metres (150 on dual carriageways or motorways) along the road, in the direction facing approaching traffic, so drivers meet it before meeting you. Get passengers out, and off the road, as someone may crash into the car. Keep children and animals under control.

If you're on the hard shoulder, get help. Follow the arrows to the nearest phone, where you can tell police you have broken down, and what motoring organisation you belong to. If you're on a normal road, and are not in an exposed position, have a look to see if you can do anything yourself. Get help if you can't. Tell police if the car's causing an obstruction.

Even if you're still moving, stop as soon as you can if oil or ignition lights stay on once you've started, or if the engine overheats, or there's knocking or smoke.

THINGS TO CARRY WITH YOU

- Spare bulbs
- Wire and tape to hold things together until you get to a garage
- Pliers for the wire
- Torch
- Brake/clutch fluid
- Bottle of water for the radiator
- Fire extinguisher
- A first aid box
- Jack (a bottle jack is easier to use than the one usually provided, but may be heavier)
- Piece of wood to stand jack on, on uneven ground
- Wheel nut spanner (a ring spanner may be better than the one provided)
- Tube for extra leverage on spanner
- Spare fan belt, preferably an emergency one for easy replacement, just to get you home (a permanent one's hard to change)

What can I do myself to get going again?

Remember everything will be hot. Firstly, check the petrol. The gauge may be stuck so take the cap off and rock the car while trying to hear fuel swishing in the tank. If the engine won't work, try opening the bonnet and seeing if there are any leads hanging off. Check that no connections are loose.

If you've overheated, you may need more water in the radiator, but **DON'T** take its cap off when it's just boiled. If there's a fire in the engine, don't open the bonnet. Release the catch and point the fire extinguisher through a tiny gap.

If you don't have a spare fan belt, an old technique is to make a temporary one out of a stocking.

Use one of your stockings

Changing a wheel

1. Put jack under car at the appropriate point. Wind until the tyre's clear of the ground
2. Take off the hub-cap
3. Use the spanner to undo the wheel nuts
4. Pull off the old wheel
5. Replace with the spare wheel
6. Replace nuts TIGHTLY (square end outwards), and put hub-cap back

Changing a wheel

WHEEL CHANGING TIPS

Get a spanner with a handle that can have a long tube put over it, to increase leverage. The handbrake won't hold front wheels, so you may need to lower the jack SLIGHTLY, to hold the tyre against the ground while you turn the nuts.

Rock the car while trying to hear fuel swishing in the tank

IF YOU HAVE AN ACCIDENT

- Stop
- Call the emergency services if anyone is hurt
- Give the other driver your name and address, those of car's owner and the number and make of car
- Get the same from other driver
- Exchange insurance details with the other driver
- If someone's been hurt, or you couldn't do the above, tell the police within 24 hours
- Draw map, take photos, make notes
- Taken names of witnesses

Most people have some small knocks during their driving career. Modern bumpers absorb a lot of energy and may be only slightly damaged, or not at all. However, you may encounter (or be involved in) a bigger crash. Help if you can but do not just slow down to look. This can cause another crash.

If you have an accident which hurts someone, or damages someone else's property, or hurts an animal like a dog or large farm animal (unless the dog or cow was in your own car), you must stop. Give your name and address and those of the car's owner, and the make and registration number of the car, to anyone who has the right to ask, for instance the other driver or a police officer. If anyone was hurt or you're blamed for some of the damage, you must give insurance details too. (You normally exchange these anyway.) If you couldn't stop, or there was no one to give details to, or you didn't have your insurance certificate with you, then contact the police in person within 24 hours. Go to them anyway if someone was hurt. Also do all this if you didn't crash but you contributed to someone else's accident. Most insurance companies say don't apologise or admit blame. Be aware, however, that if both of you know you're the one to blame for a bump, not saying sorry with good grace will make the situation more tense.

Take similar details from the other driver, plus the names of witnesses. Take a photo of the scene if you can. Draw a map and pace out distances. Note down weather and road conditions, injuries and any

If you hurt an animal you must stop

other relevant details. If someone won't give the details they should, take their car's registration number and contact the police.

If you're first at the accident scene, remember that no one should risk their own safety; you cannot help if you are also injured. Warn others by using hazard warning lights and a red triangle. Switch off engines and don't let anyone smoke. Tell those uninjured to move away from the scene. Call the emergency services immediately or send someone to call. Don't move the injured unless they're in more danger remaining where they are (perhaps from fire) than aggravating an injury, especially to neck, back or head. Don't remove a motorcyclist's helmet unless you absolutely must. Give first aid if you can. Stay until the emergency teams arrive, and tell them the facts.

If a lorry with dangerous load markings is involved, don't go near it. Note any details of the markings and tell the emergency services when you phone (so what is needed can be brought without delay).

AVOIDING ACCIDENTS

The best way to avoid accidents is to drive carefully with good anticipation, at a speed that would let you stop within the distance you can see. All the normal rules apply. Be aware that others may not always be driving as carefully. Rely on seeing trouble early enough to deal with it, and on letting others know you're there. On a single-track road, you may meet oncoming cars. Drive slowly and honk to warn anyone you can't see who probably can't see you either. Take extra care on bends, humpback bridges and other places where you can't see far ahead.

If you see warning triangles or hazard warning lights, or there is slow-moving traffic ahead, then slow down and be ready to stop. Brake early and gently. Use hazard warning lights if you stop.

PROCEDURE AT A CRASH SCENE

- Never put your own life at risk
- Warn others by using hazard lights, red triangles etc.
- No smoking and engines off
- Call emergency services. Give all relevant information and mention any hazardous load labels
- Don't approach a hazardous load
- Don't move injured unless at risk
- Don't remove motorcycle helmets
- Give first aid if you can
- Get the uninjured away from road

Warn others

SAFETY FEATURES

Modern cars include many features to help you survive a crash. Most important are the seat belts, which halve your risk of death or serious injury. Children need special restraints suitable for their size and should always use them. It is your responsibility. Apart from drivers who are reversing, people in cars MUST use seat belts, if there are any, unless they have medical exemption certificates.

Head-restrains must also be used correctly. They stop your head being jerked back in a collision, protecting your neck from whiplash. They must be adjusted for your head. They are not neck-rests.

The windscreen may be either toughened or laminated glass. Toughened glass shatters into tiny cubes. These aren't sharp like normal broken glass, but can cut; also you can't see through a windscreen in this state. If it doesn't fall out, make a hole to see through by pushing out the glass with a piece of wood or a thoroughly protected hand – toughened glass breaks away easily when shattered. A laminated windscreen has a layer of plastic between layers of glass. It'll probably stay in one piece and you'll be able to see through it, though any pieces that do fall off may be sharp.

THE DRIVING TEST

There are two parts to the test: the practical and the theory. Your instructor will tell you when and how to apply. The test makes sure people can drive safely before being let out alone in control of a ton of speeding car. Perfection isn't expected. A few small faults won't fail you, but a single error that endangers people will. Qualified drivers often make such errors (e.g. not using the mirror enough) but at least they've proved they can drive safely if they try.

Make sure the car's clean and working well. Take your provisional licence (signed in ink) and your glasses if you use them. Remember that many test centres don't have toilets! Drive there yourself and arrive about 15 minutes early. When your time comes, the examiner will call your name and get you to sign a form. Then he'll ask you to lead the way to your car. On the way he'll get you to do the eyesight test by reading a number-plate further away than the law demands, using glasses if you drive in them. If you can't do it, the distance will be measured exactly. If you still can't do it, you'll fail, but otherwise you'll go to the car. Wait for the examiner to get in before doing your cockpit drill, so he knows you've done it. You'll be allowed to drive for a little while to settle down, before being tested on the emergency stop.

The eyesight test

The rest may be in any order. Most of the points the examiner is looking for won't be specifically tested but will be watched throughout the test. You **will** be tested on two out of these three: reverse into an opening, reverse park, turn in the road.

The examiner will only say enough to tell you what to do, because small talk may distract you. He may write things down during the test but don't worry. The test lasts about 35 minutes (or 70 for the retest of a driver convicted of an automatic disqualification offence).

At the end, he'll say how you did and give you a copy of the test report. If you've failed, he'll briefly explain why. If you've passed, he'll give you a pass certificate; this means you can drive on your own, without L-plates, straight away. Either way, let your instructor drive you home. If you fail, then apply for another test immediately.

If you pass, get the application form for a full licence. You can drive while waiting for the licence, but note down your driver number and the date you passed before sending off the certificate.

Your first drive alone will feel odd. There's no one to help out. It's all down to you. Start on quiet roads and take things easy.

If you've failed, he'll briefly explain why

Items you will be tested on

I have discussed these elsewhere in the book, but here's the test as the examiner sees it (the topics he will make notes about), together with some points to bear in mind.

EYESIGHT You must be able to read number-plate letters 79.4 mm high from 20.5 metres.

CHECKS BEFORE STARTING ENGINE Once examiner is in car, check: Mirrors? Doors shut? Seat belt on? Handbrake on? Neutral gear?

USING THE CONTROLS CORRECTLY Especially clutch, steering, gears, accelerator, brakes. Know what everything does or means.

MOVING OFF Safely and under control, on flat, on hills, at an angle.

EMERGENCY STOP The examiner warns you, then gives a signal. Stop quickly, safely and under control, without the wheels locking.

REVERSING INTO AN OPENING To right or left, under control, and with regard for others.

REVERSE PARKING Within about two car lengths behind a parked car. Stop close to kerb.

TURNING IN ROAD Using forward and reverse gears, under control, with regard for others.

USE OF MIRRORS Before ANY manoeuvre (including opening doors). Only move your eyes not your whole head. Act on what you see.

GIVING SIGNALS Only use the signals in the Highway Code. Make sure indicators cancel.

ACTING ON SIGNS, SIGNALS AND MARKINGS Act on them all, when following road ahead.

MAKING PROGRESS Don't go too slow, or stop at junctions when you don't need to.

FOLLOWING BEHIND VEHICLES The two-second rule; braking distances.

CARE IN THE USE OF SPEED Don't go too fast for speed limits or conditions.

ROAD JUNCTIONS (including roundabouts): Use MSM/PSL. Don't cut corners. Wait for bikes and pedestrians. Use correct lane.

OVERTAKING/MEETING/CROSSING PATH OF OTHERS Do it safely. Give bikes and horses plenty of room.

POSITION ON THE ROAD Keep left, but don't drive in the gutter. Use correct lane.

PASSING STATIONARY VEHICLES Allow adequate clearance, a door's width if possible.

PEDESTRIAN CROSSINGS Be considerate and courteous to pedestrians. Give arm signal if safe (have window open on test, if possible).

SELECTING A SAFE POSITION for normal stops: Ensure you won't be an obstruction or a hazard. Stop close to the kerb.

AWARENESS AND ANTICIPATION Be aware of others. Plan ahead and be ready for dangers.

The theory test

Before you take your practical test, you must pass the theory test. Having passed the theory test you can try the practical as many times as you like, but if you still haven't passed it after two years you'll have to do the theory again.

The test will last for 40 minutes, during which time you have to answer 35 multiple-choice questions. Most questions require one answer to be chosen from four alternatives; some ask for two or three from more than four, and these are indicated on the paper. The test is available in a variety of languages and arrangements can be made for people with special needs.

Questions will cover alertness, attitude, vehicle faults and the environment, weather and road conditions, perception, judgement, other road users, other vehicles, own vehicle handling, motorways, other roads, signs and signals, documents, accident handling, vehicle loading and accident risk. Learn your Highway Code; practise and think about your driving skills and you will find that all these elements are part of learning to drive well.

FINDING YOUR WAY

The main object of having a car is to get you somewhere. Knowing how to drive along and turn corners etc. is all very well but it's useless if you don't know where you're going. People do most of their driving on familiar routes; so take the time before setting off on an unfamiliar one to make sure you are prepared. Remember that you will need to concentrate harder on where you are going on unknown roads, while still maintaining the same level of attention on the driving itself.

Before taking an unfamiliar route, make sure demisters, wipers, lights etc. are working. Check that tyres are correctly inflated, and you have sufficient oil and petrol.

Use a map to plan the journey before you go. Make brief notes and put them where you can see them while driving. Include things like the name of the road before the one you want (as a warning). For motorways you can list the junction numbers and just look for these. Where there are no numbers you can see junctions in terms of road numbers and destinations. So if your journey includes going a certain distance east along the A127, then your note for the roundabout may be 'Take A127 towards Southend' even though you don't actually want to go there.

Don't forget to take the map and the address of your destination with you. A compass and a passenger to navigate can also be handy.

IF YOU ARE LOST

Continue driving carefully, taking the major road at each junction until you get to one that has the road signs to say where you are. Stop safely and check your map before continuing your journey in the right direction.

If you have a compass, stop the car safely and take a compass bearing. Turn the map to point the correct way and focus on the area in which you are situated. Look around you for things that might appear on the map (on an Ordnance Survey there's lots of detail to choose from) and try to locate them on the map itself. Cross-check with a number of features. Work out your new route before proceeding safely.

The environment and the car

Motor vehicles are responsible for 20 per cent of the UK's carbon dioxide air pollution, and this is the most common greenhouse gas. They also add lead, carbon monoxide and nitrogen oxide to the atmosphere, emit soot, and the increasing numbers demand more and more roads. Actually making cars creates pollution. So what can we do to use our cars in a sensible way? There are no easy answers; even some of the modern 'solutions' are controversial.

When choosing a car, select one which has the most environmentally friendly features, has a catalytic converter, if possible, and uses unleaded petrol or diesel. A catalytic convertor (or CAT) removes most of the nitrogen oxide, carbon monoxide and hydrocarbons from exhaust fumes, but does not cut carbon dioxide. CATs, however, don't work well when the car has just started on cold mornings.

Unleaded petrol must be used on cars with CATs and can be used on most other cars. However, critics point out that it does contain more benzene than leaded petrol. Diesel fuel is often considered better than petrol as it reduces emissions. Do choose a fuel-efficient car.

Have your car regularly serviced. It has to pass the MOT exhaust-emissions test. If it is well maintained and the tyres are at the correct pressure, emissions are lessened. Dispose of old tyres and oil properly.

Only drive if you must. For short journeys, walk or cycle. For longer ones, consider the bus, tram or train.

Drive at steady and sensible speeds and avoid hard braking and acceleration; the rule is 'quality rather than quantity'. Driving at 50 mph uses considerably less fuel than driving at 70 mph. Extra weight or extra drag, created by a roof-rack, for example, burns more fuel and alters handling.

PAPERWORK AND THE LAW

Road traffic law is there to protect you. Read the law section in the Highway Code. The law also appears throughout the code, wherever you are told, 'you must'. Even where it isn't the law, obey the Highway Code.

There are several documents a driver needs. Make sure you have everything necessary to make your car-driving legal.

DRIVING LICENCE

As a learner you need a provisional licence. After you pass, you exchange it for a full licence which lasts until you're 70. After 70, you need a new one every three years (but you don't have to take the test again). Visitors can drive for a year on a foreign licence.

INSURANCE

You must be insured to drive what you drive. If the car is someone else's this normally means their insurance must cover you too, but if it's yours you'll have to arrange your own. The minimum legal insurance is 'third party'. This pays for damage you do to others. More expensive are 'third party, fire and theft' and 'comprehensive' (the best). It will often cost more if you're young, or if you drive a powerful car. People with certain occupations also pay more. Different companies' rates vary, so shop around. You get a certificate of insurance which you should carry with you. You'll also get a policy which explains the details. Leave this at home.

MOT CERTIFICATE

(Vehicle test certificate): Once your car is over three years old it must have an MOT test every year. This checks its safety and environmental impact. You can have the car tested up to a month before the certificate expires, and the new one will continue from the old one's end. Carry the certificate with you. If the car fails the test, you can have it fixed and re-tested.

VEHICLE REGISTRATION DOCUMENT

This carries details of the car and its owner. When you buy a second-hand car you must fill in the change of owner section and send it to DVLA.

VEHICLE EXCISE DUTY

(Road fund licence or Road tax): This is the disc displayed in the lower left of the windscreen. It must be renewed every year (or six months), usually at a post office. To get it you need to show your certificate of insurance and your MOT. You will also need a completed application form and the fee.

CONTINENTAL DRIVING

The fines for speeding are often heavy

As our connections with Europe become closer, more and more people are driving on the Continent. There are many things – such as different regulations, route planning, medical insurance, special equipment that must be carried – to consider. If you join a motoring organisation it can help you with all of these. It can also assist in case you break down in a foreign country. To help prevent the breakdown itself, have the car serviced before going.

It may sound obvious, but never forget that most other countries drive on the right. Use all your mirrors before any manoeuvre. Think what you're doing even more carefully than usual, especially at roundabouts. Your car will also have to be adjusted: your lights need deflectors so you don't dazzle people (the headlights will dip the wrong way), and make sure your left door mirror is properly adjusted. Most countries require third-party insurance. Your policy probably covers this, but check. Some countries outside the European Union, still require an International Driving Permit (consult your motoring organisation). Most countries don't let you drive until you're 18.

Keep valuables hidden, even if you're in the car. Beware: there are cities where the criminals not only steal your radio, but where they don't even have the decency to run away afterwards. You may meet them when you return to the car. Keep a separate note of your passport number and its date and place of issue, in case it's lost or stolen.

Many motoring offences carry on-the-spot fines. The fines for speeding are often heavy. The penalties for drink-driving may be even more severe than in the UK. Don't squeeze any more passengers into the car than it was designed for, and use your seat belt.

THINGS YOU SHOULD TAKE
Most of these are compulsory somewhere. Even where they aren't, they're a good idea
- Driving licence (and possibly International Driving Permit)
- Vehicle registration document
- Emergency repair kit
- First-aid kit
- Spares kit (spare bulbs, at least, are often compulsory)
- Emergency windscreen
- Advance warning triangle (some countries require two)
- Fire extinguisher
- The normal wheel-changing tools
- Nationality plate (you must have this)

Unless you're lucky enough to have lots of money or rich generous relatives, your first car will probably be a used one. Used cars are OK, but you must be careful. A reputable dealer may give the best after-care, with an impressive guarantee but check how long it lasts and what's covered. An auction's cheaper but you have fewer rights, so check the terms and conditions of sale. Trickiest of all are private sales, but there's still no reason why you shouldn't get a good car this way, possibly very cheaply. Just be extra strict about taking precautions. It's important to get an independent expert to check the car. Motoring organisations provide this service, or you can pay a mechanic to do it. Before a test drive, check the insurance covers you and the MOT and tax are up to date. Check the mileage and number of owners, and make sure there are no finance or hire purchase agreements outstanding. Ask why the car is being sold.

The car may have 'filler' (plastic cement used to fill holes, then painted over) where rust's been ground away or where there's been a dent. This isn't a problem with a cheap old car, but on a fairly new one it may indicate it's been in a crash. Take a small magnet (covered in a cloth so you don't scratch the paint) when you go to see the car, and find places where it's not attracted to the bodywork, where it may be meeting

Take a small magnet when you go to see the car

filler rather than metal. This won't work on fibreglass or aluminium bodies, which don't attract magnets. Bounce each corner. If it bounces more than twice on its own after you've stopped pushing, there may be suspension trouble. Warm up the engine and listen for noises. Blue exhaust smoke is trouble.

There are disreputable dealers, unfortunately, who may turn back the milometer or weld sections of two cars together. Only buy from dealers with a sound reputation. If in doubt, don't buy.

When you get a car, especially an old one, it may require more maintenance, or work to get it through the MOT. Not always true, but buy one with a long time left on its certificate, just in case.

Remember as you buy that bargain, that you must add the cost of insurance, road tax, MOT, maintenance, petrol. A car's like a hole in the road that you pour money into, but most of us feel it's worth it for the privilege of just going wherever we decide to go.

Blue exhaust smoke is trouble

THEORY TEST

QUESTIONS

1 What does a sign with a broken black circle in a red triangle mean?

a) Mini-roundabout
b) Roundabout
c) One-way system
d) No bicycles

2 You have just overtaken another car. Should you:

a) Exceed the speed limit to get well ahead

b) Move back to the left when you see the other car in your mirror

c) Move back to the left when you are just past the other car

d) Stay on the right until you are ten car lengths ahead

3 Parked cars on a residential road leave room for a single line of traffic. The speed limit is 30 mph. What is the safe speed.

a) 30 mph   b) About 35 mph
c) About 25 mph   d) Under 20 mph

4 A motorcycle may surprise you by:

a) Going through a red light
b) Stopping suddenly
c) Driving without lights
d) Swerving suddenly

5 What should you do if your car starts to skid?

a) Turn the opposite way to the skid
b) Brake hard
c) Turn into the skid
d) Select a lower gear

6 By how much may ice increase the normal stopping distance?

a) 10 times   b) 2 times
c) 5 times   d) 70 times

7 Who has priority at an unmarked junction

a) The traffic on the widest road
b) The fastest traffic
c) The traffic on the busiest road
d) Nobody

8 How long after registration must a car have its first MOT test?

a) 12 months   b) 18 months
c) 3 years   d) 5 years

9 Which type of exhaust pollution is not cut by a catalytic converter?

a) Carbon monoxide
b) Carbon dioxide
c) Nitrogen oxide
d) Hydrocarbons

10 Which of these combinations of tyres are not safe? (pick 2)

a) Radial-ply at the front and cross-ply at the rear

b) Radial-ply at the rear and cross-ply at the front

c) Radial-ply all round

d) Cross-ply all round

e) Cross-ply on one side and radial-ply on the other

11 Which of these is most likely to impair your judgement?

a) Smoking
b) Prescription drugs
c) Eating cream cakes
d) Wearing glasses

By how much may ice increase the normal stopping distance?

12 What does a sign with a steam engine in a red triangle mean?

a) Level crossing without gates or barriers

b) Level crossing with manual gates

c) Any level crossing

d) Railway station

13 Which of these does not increase fuel consumption?

a) Hard braking

b) Hard acceleration

c) Driving fast

d) Having the heater on

14 What is the sequence of colours at traffic lights?

a) Red, Red and Amber, Green, Amber, Red

b) Red, Amber, Green, Red and Amber, Red

c) Red, Amber, Green, Amber, Red

d) Red, Green, Amber, Red

15 In good conditions, how many seconds' gap should you leave to the car in front?

a) 1   b) 2

c) 3   d) 4

16 A motorcyclist is lying in the road following an accident, and is complaining of a headache. Do you:

a) Remove his helmet

b) Call an ambulance

c) Give him an asprin

d) Ignore him

17 You have just driven through a ford. How do you dry your brakes?

a) Drive fast so the air rushes over them

b) Pull to the side of the road until they dry off

c) Dry them with clean tissue

d) Drive slowly while breaking gently

You have just driven through a ford. How do you dry your brakes?

18 What do you do if the vehicle behind is too close?

a) Ease your speed upwards to increase the gap behind you again

b) Ease your speed down to increase the gap in front of you

c) Brake gently so he sees the brake light and backs off

d) Do nothing but be extra careful

19 What position do you wait in when you want to turn right?

a) To the right of your lane so traffic can pass on your left

b) To the left of your lane so traffic can pass on your right

c) Straddling the centre of the road so you don't impede traffic

d) On the other side of the road so you can see oncoming traffic

20 When driving past horses you should... (pick 3)

a) Go fast to get by them quickly

b) Go slow so that you don't alarm them

c) Honk your horn to let the rider know you are coming

d) Don't sound your horn

e) Don't rev your engine

21
What does a sign with a diagonal black bar on a white circle mean?

a) Speed derestricted
b) No entry for vehicular traffic
c) No stopping (clearway)
d) National speed limit applies

22 Which of the following are allowed on the motorway? (pick 2)

a) Large motorcycles
b) Caravans
c) Learner car drivers
d) Large animals
e) Fast tractors

23 What is the drill before a manoeuvre?

a) Mirror, signal, position, speed, look
b) Signal, mirror, position, speed, look
c) Mirror, position, signal, speed, turn
d) Mirror, position, speed, look, signal

24 You park your car pointing up hill. There is no kerb. Which way should the front wheels be pointing?

a) Straight ahead
b) Towards the edge of the road
c) Away from the edge of the road
d) Any way that lets you move off quickly

What is not a colour for catseyes?

25 What is not a colour for Catseyes?

a) Red
b) Amber
c) Blue
d) Green

26 When cornering on snow should you...? (pick 3)

a) Slip the clutch
b) Avoid the clutch
c) Brake gently all the way round
d) Avoid braking on the bend
e) Steer smoothly

27 If your engine overheats should you:

a) Immediately remove the radiator cap
b) Leave removing the radiator cap to a trained mechanic
c) Call a motoring organisation
d) Wait for the engine to cool naturally

28 Meeting another vehicle at night, where should you dip your headlights earlier?

a) On a hill
b) On a right-hand bend
c) On a left-hand bend
d) Where the road is narrow

29 What unusual thing may an articulated lorry do before turning left at a junction?

a) Stop and reverse slightly
b) Hoot to warn people to get out of the way
c) Swing out to the right
d) Stop so that the driver can assess the junction

30 There is an area of road marked with diagonal white lines and surrounded by a solid white line. What does this mean?

a) Do not enter unless you can see your exit is clear
b) Wait here when you intend to turn right
c) You should not enter the area unless you can see it is safe
d) You must not enter the area except in an emergency

What can you use the motorway hard shoulder for?

31 Who is responsible for seeing that 14 year old passengers use their seat belts?

a) They are responsible for themselves
b) Their parents are responsible
c) The driver is responsible
d) The police are responsible

32 Which of these may you overtake? (pick 3)

a) A parked car where there are double solid white lines
b) Traffic on your right when everyone is moving slowly in queues
c) Traffic on your right that is moving at 28 mph
d) A car on your right that is indicating a right turn
e) Traffic near an empty zebra crossing

33 Your car full of passengers has broken down on a level crossing. What is the FIRST thing you do?

a) Use the railway telephone to inform the signal operator
b) Get your passengers out and clear of the crossing

c) Get yourself clear of the crossing
d) Move your vehicle off the crossing

34 Where should you position yourself on a right-hand bend?

a) To the left of your lane
b) To the right of your lane, near the centre of the road
c) In the middle of your lane
d) From left to right to left, so you take a gentler curve

35 What can you use the motorway hard shoulder for?

a) Answering the phone
b) Waiting for a breakdown truck
c) Having something to eat
d) Resting if you are very tired

ANSWERS

1: b	**10:** ae	**19:** a	**28:** c
2: b	**11:** b	**20:** bde	**29:** c
3: d	**12:** a	**21:** d	**30:** d
4: d	**13:** d	**22:** ab	**31:** a
5: c	**14:** a	**23:** a	**32:** abd
6: a	**15:** b	**24:** b	**33:** b
7: d	**16:** b	**25:** c	**34:** a
8: c	**17:** d	**26:** bde	**35:** b
9: b	**18:** b	**27:** d	

CONCLUSION

There! Now you know everything about driving ... dream on! What you have if you remember everything your instructor taught you, all this book and the Highway Code, is the basics. But it's with practice and experience that the real learning happens.

After you've passed the test, even 50 years after, there'll still be new situations to face. But if you have a sound understanding of the principles and apply your knowledge and common sense, then you can become a better and better driver. So drive safely and responsibly, and never forget to ENJOY.

There'll still be new situations to face